Where Icarus Failed to Fly

Where Icarus Failed to Fly

William and Emily Andrews

WHERE ICARUS FAILED TO FLY

iUniverse books may be ordered through booksellers or by contacting:

iUniverse
1663 Liberty Drive
Bloomington, IN 47403
www.iuniverse.com
1-800-Authors (1-800-288-4677)

Because of the dynamic nature of the internet, any web addresses or links contained in this book may have changed since publication and may no longer be valid. The views expressed in this work are solely those of the author and do not necessarily reflect the views of the publisher, and the publisher hereby disclaims any responsibility for them.

Any people depicted in stock imagery provided by Getty Images are models, and such images are being used for illustrative purposes only.
Certain stock imagery © Getty Images.

ISBN: 978-1-5320-4399-4 (sc)
ISBN: 978-1-5320-4400-7 (e)

Library of Congress Control Number: 2018902360

Print information available on the last page.

iUniverse rev. date: 03/29/2018

Contents

PART 1

PART 2

To my beloved grandmother "in lieu of lemon pudding"

Preface

WILLIAM AND I came from backgrounds of academic success where answers and solutions to everyday problems easily materialized for ourselves and for our clients. William, a theologian, believed God would always be present and together all things could be conquered. "Casting all your cares on Him for He careth for you" (1 Peter 5:7). He prayed for God to focus his spirit to surrender his need to solve his problems alone. He saw any disbelief as a detour from his confidence that God shared his concerns and had already provided the avenues through which the needed answers would come.

Each day, we prayed his personal prayer: "Holy Spirit, I lay all my cares before You, surrendering all attachments to them in the confidence that out of all things You will bring good, if only I trust. Thanking Thee, Holy Spirit, eternal Father, for all the evidences of Thy constancy and benevolence, I commend my spirit, my life, unto Thee. Use me for Thy glory. Amen."

Until our experience at the inn, as the following story reveals, we easily surrendered our lives to God, laying our lives at His feet and offering each and every moment to Him. But the secrets, the frustration, and the elusive hold on our reality gave way to doubt, insecurity, helplessness, and sometimes the pain of losing our way to God. The clouds of our emotional and physical needs obscured the face of the Divine. Our shattered nerves were slowly moving us from our commitment to surrender to God's will and purpose. Each existential moment, when we should have been relying on God's promise of His eternal presence, was lost to the anxiety of what we feared was the next unimaginable, unbelievable difficulty we would have to face. We prayed for God's forgiveness to restore our sanity to a centered spirit and guide us into His encompassing love and peace.

The universe answered. William suffered a massive cardiac event—one from which no surgeon would or could predict he could survive. With nowhere else to turn, it became patently obvious God had given us what turned out to be the miracle extricating us from the evil under which we'd been living for those years. When visiting William in the hospital, I told him he didn't need to be sick for this problem to be solved. It did, however, change our circumstances and the rest of our lives.

For four months of hospitalization, the constancy of God's presence was obvious. One Saturday night, the medical team informed me I would need to make a decision to discontinue William's life support because of complications from which they were sure he could not recover. At that moment, I witnessed a bright spirit ascending from the upper half of William's body. As I prayed, his spirit descended and returned to his mortal coil. As I sat by his bedside, caressing him, I felt a hand touch my right shoulder. The quiet, soothing voice of the Divine said, "Little one, everything will be well." In spite of the four months needed for recovery, William was discharged physically and spiritually whole.

William lived fourteen more years and died in my arms from complications from his heart attack. During those years, we lived our faith in thanksgiving for God's blessings. William touched the lives of thousands through his selfless acts of kindness and generosity of spirit. Each day, my husband lived a life that was, for me, the proof of God's existence. He is an extraordinary being.

Completing our book is my promise. It began while William was recovering from his heart attack. While regaining his strength, we spent all our time creating. There was only a fleeting thought that it might be published one day. In fact, the original manuscript traveled many miles for many years at the bottom of a box of pictures, spiritual books, and William's theological writings only to have recently surfaced. It was only at the urging of friends and family who recognized the positive impact our story might have that I began to pursue publishing this manuscript.

Offering my thanksgiving for this opportunity to fulfill my life's purpose and my feelings of profound sorrow brings me closer to God. He shares and understands the ache in my heart and is already providing the avenues through which the needed peace will come. Admittedly, my courage and strength fails me many times during the day, and my sobs rise from the depths of my soul. But then a friendly hand and heart reach out to hold me up. A voice says, "I love you." I know, somehow, it is honest and sincere, a moment to help me cope just one more minute.

Each day, I ask God to place on my path a soul in whose life I can make a difference—even a small one. He has never failed me. I ask for a message from my husband—an image, a song, a bird, tired clouds on a mountain face, or the amazing dreams when I am held in his arms until I awaken to the reality he can only stay for a moment. I hold on to God's promise that we will be reunited when I am called home. Until then, I must be satisfied to freely soar where Icarus failed to fly, sharing the sweetness of his mystic presence and the constancy of his psychic touch. For now, this is my reality—and he remains my life.

Introduction

WHAT FOLLOWS IS a story, together with my psychological and theological analysis, of evil and its handmaidens: ego and economics. It is a story that encompasses four years (with some historic digressions) in the lives of me and my wife. It begins with an adventure, walks through that valley where "the shadows of death lie heavily across their pathways" (Psalm 23:4), and culminates in a soteriological victory.

This victory—credited to the principles of love and truth guiding my wife, Emily, and me through our lives and especially through the torturous meanderings of these several years—are best summarized in 1 Corinthians 13, which I have translated from Greek:

> Suppose I was able to speak all earthly languages,
> And even understood angelic communications,
> Without love I sound like a clanging gong or a tinkling cymbal;
> Even were I gifted in prophesy
> Understanding all mysteries,
> Acquainted with all knowledge,
> Then, in addition I had sufficient faith to remove mountains,
> But do not have love all of this is nothing;
> I might surrender everything to feed the poor,
> Give my body as a sacrifice,
> But have not love
> All this is worthless,
> Love is longsuffering and kind,
> Love is never envious,
> Love is not arrogant or proud,
> Love does not behave in peevish or pouting ways,
> Love refuses to think evil of anyone,
> Love does not rejoice at the misfortunes of others,
> Love revels only in the truth,
> Love bears all things,

Believes all things,
Hopes always;
There is no end to love;
Prophecies fail,
Languages change,
Knowledge disappears,
Because all of these are limited,
Only Truth is eternal.
As a child, I thought like a child,
Understood as a child,
But when I matured,
I put away my infantile ways.
For, now, we see through a dirty windowpane;
But when the light of Truth is come,
The pane will become clear.
Now my knowledge is limited,
My prophesy, imperfect and partial;
But, eventually, I will see God face to face;
Then, I will know even as I am known,
There are three great gifts in the world:
Faith,
Hope,
Love;
But, by far, the greatest of these is
Love.

The Greek word *agape* is often translated as *charity*, the highest form of love possible. Agape (love) is ascribable only to God; it is that trait of the Deity toward which human beings are encouraged to aspire. To be possessed by this love, to surrender to it, is the key to possessing that love in whatever way we are humanly capable. Like the manna in the wilderness (a gift vouchsafed daily and repeated daily to the itinerate Jews), this love event is an existential experience, the process for which is described in the latter chapters of this book.

In direct opposition to this process eventuating the good is the Hebraic understanding of evil: the Ten Commandments thundered to Moses at

Sinai. These were not ten laws but ten aspects of a single command: "Thou shalt have no other Gods before me" (Exodus 20:2–7).

The ensuing chapters are indices of the ways in which human beings disavow allegiance to God. The Hebrew word for *evil* is Ra (whether this is a reference to the worship of the Egyptian deity of the same name is open to conjecture). It means "to break into pieces." There is only one sin: disobedience to God. Everything else in the Ten Commandments and in the Old Testament referring to evil is commentary on the ways we "break into pieces" that single commandment. If surrender to the love of God is the way to light and peace (agape), then evil is the complete absence of surrender to the Deity: a "breaking into pieces" of the primal union between God and humankind.

The names of those who populate these pages have been changed to protect the guilty. Are the evil events herein described exaggerated? Possibly. Are they real? Maybe not—but you will need to decide.

To live in the midst of mystery is one of God's greatest gifts. To dare the question and brave its unanswered extensions is the first article of faith. There are no road maps, no directional signs, and no asking, "Are we there yet?"

There is just the journey and the dark. Whether it is a frightening velvet blackness, empty and void, or the soft exhilaration of companionship depends on our expectations for the journey and with whom we walk.

PART 1

In the beginning, the Gods created the heavens and
the earth; now that earth was empty and void, a chaos,
darkness; an awesome wind swept across the abyss.
—Genesis 1:1–2

Chapter 1

The Adventure Begins

I T WAS DARK. An inky blackness draped itself over the world like a velvet shroud, like the one that cloaks the crucifix on Black Saturday. Streetlights appeared as pinpoints through this enshrouding blackness; car lights through this veil danced like miniature banshees summoning the world to its demise. The dark was not merely an indication of the time of day. It was a mythic conjuring of those black sisters who waylaid Macbeth and Banquo, prophesying doom for the Thane of Cawdor. It was a dark like that to which theologians and philosophers refer to as the "dark night of the soul," a darkness of evil and immoral proportions referenced by the holy evangelists in their retelling of the Last Supper: "And Judas went out, and it was night."

To most of the peoples of the world—with their inherent psychological pessimism, psychiatric depression, narcissistic desires, and sociopathic propensities—this dark was unnoticeable and normal. There are few people with the moral insight capable of distinguishing that darkness from truth and light. There is both a subconscious and conscious hatred by those whose darkness is complete toward those who scale the precipices that lead to light. Plato describes, in his cave analogy, how the masses live in the depths of the cave among the darkness and shadows, angered by those "fools" intent on climbing the craggy slopes to the cave entrance, where the light of pure truth resides.

My wife, Emily, and I—innocent in our naïveté of the immensity of the blackness into which we had been driving—descended into that night. The incline was gradual; only wisps of fog and clouds were initially our companions. My father and mother, for whom we had cared in their illnesses for several years, had just died, one month apart, after seventy-two years of marriage. A brand-new adventure awaited us. With a few of their possessions and some of ours in a rented truck, we drove unexpectedly into a small town where, unknown to us, the mystic powers from the

1

netherworld's coven were already at work. As the shade of evening began to surround us, we entered the parking lot of a small inn. We were greeted by small, swarthy people whose form and visages would eventually subsume within and become indistinguishable from that evil blackness that would become our souls' dark night within a few short years.

The inn, one of the few in the area, accepted our cat, Clifford. We decided to rent a small room in the front building from the manager and his wife. As I backed the rented truck into the space in front of our room, I inadvertently hit part of the roof's drip edge. Even as I was climbing down from my truck, with crossed arms and a face clouded in midnight gloom, there stood the manager, angered that his roof had been damaged. Immediately, Emily told him that I could fix almost anything. He seemed, at best, pessimistic. I found a few tools, climbed on the bed of the truck, and repaired the damage. When I had finished, he examined the repair with grim satisfaction and stalked back to his office. I closed the truck.

Emily and I entered our small room and our dark night, lasting three and three-quarter years. We descended into a night of conjured magic, evil portents, and mystic shadows.

Edgar Allan Poe's "Descent into a Maelstrom" describes the slow movement, almost imperceptible, at the edges of a whirlpool. With irresistible force and frighteningly accelerating velocity, one is pulled down and into the dark, suffocating center of the vortex to ultimate death. So was the beginning of our maelstrom.

We arrived armed with enthusiasm, talents, education, and little money. My parents' illnesses absorbed all but the small savings we carried with us. The next morning, we began the process of settling our lives. With the image of repairing the roof under the heading of opportunity, I was approached with the suggestion that there were some jobs about the inn that I might do. I proposed helping him in exchange for our accommodations. I kept a running tab of projects: labor hours at the current market value minus the cost of the room. Shortly, my salary was far exceeding the rent. Agreeing the difference would be paid when we checked out, I viewed this as money in the bank.

He asked each day if I were capable of performing some new task—from repairing deck chairs to hanging vinyl siding. All these requests seemed innocent. We were in transition, we possessed the requisite skills, and we were simply saving money and temporarily earning a place to live. Before too long, the projects became more and more extensive, sometimes taking two or three weeks to complete. Inevitably, before the current job was completed, he had ordered the necessary materials for the subsequent beautifying improvement. So, our whirlpool began, its malignancy cloaked by our innocence, its inexorable motion toward darkness, its evil motivation and intent unnoticed.

The resident managers of the inn—and the obscure cell within which we would eventually find ourselves suffocated and bound—are described in contemporary psychological jargon. As a society, we collude to agree on the use of psychological designations for behaviors. It is one way to avoid the identification and labeling of the evil actions of which some personalities are capable. It is unpleasant, if not frightening, to recognize the actual existence of evil that controls the lives and psyches of so many people. Every day, men and women take up their occupations in private practices (doctors, lawyers, therapists, etc.) or in powerful legal and governmental positions (judges, senators, CEOs, etc.) without realizing how psychologically impaired they really are.

The pervasive destruction associated with alcohol abuse is a tragedy with which we are not only acquainted, but we welcome gladly into our lives. One wonders how many lives lie in the hands of individuals either partially inebriated or hungover from their latest cocktail lunch or evening binge. How many surgeons, whose steady hand with a scalpel is of the utmost necessity, have slipped, causing permanent damage or even death to one of their patients?

How seriously do judges and juries, burdened by their own prejudices, transferences, and need for power and control take the awesome task of deciding a defendant's fate? Or do they take delight in the misfortunes of their charge? How often does the anger associated with breakfast table miscommunication infect the decisions of those whose responsibility are the laws of our land? These examples are among many cited regarding the suffering that so easily invades our human society. We have chosen to find psychological principles and maladies to explain this antisocial conduct rather than its more real ascription: demonic evil.

Terms like *passive-aggressive, manic-depressive,* and *narcissistic-socio-pathology* are psychological and psychiatric indications that psychic professions have devised to identify various moods for the purposes of collecting insurance payments while missing the true dreadfulness of those persons so possessed. Many of these aberrant mental-health characteristics were evident in the behaviors of the manager and his wife. But identifying their character traits, as my training and experience as a psychologist directed, caused me to miss the significance of the meanness these two were capable of—an evil woven amidst the fires of hell by the angel of death, my ex-wife. She had recruited them with promises of financial gain and access to the good life. Secure within our little room, we felt little fear of the pervading darkness, the threatening storm, and the souls' depredation this unholy alliance would wreak. This horrific storm, while exacerbated by the psychological maladies these individuals projected, did not occasion their wraithlike propensities. Unaware, my wife and I attempted normal living.

While fulfilling our agreed tasks to maintain our security, we actively sought other employment. Each contact brought positive results, job interviews, and offers. But as the days rolled by, negative factors intervened: deliberately withheld phone calls, messages, and mail. Prospective employers were told we were unavailable or that we no longer resided at the inn. Initially, some of these mishaps appeared to be coincidental, but ultimately, every pursuit and pathway of escape was thwarted. The strength behind the effort was intended to totally suffocate us. With little understanding the extent of this metastatic evil and the monstrous intent that constantly enveloped us, we naively continued our quest for alternatives to the small room in the small inn in which we were confined.

Each day, the troublesome manager leveled new demands on our time, our energy, and our talents. He was small, a height not reaching the average of five feet six inches, arms and legs thin and weak, looking as if they might break with the slightest pressure. A round, dark face contained round, dark eyes that never creased in the corners with a smile. They always remained expressionless to hide a mind unable to grasp logic, a heart inured to love, and a personality warped by greed, arrogance, and mean smallness. On the surface, it was difficult to imagine that this simple immigrant harbored such a dark and malevolent soul.

His wife, standing slightly taller than her husband, also sprouted arms and legs that looked incapable of mobilizing her anorexic frame. Her face, a classic example of her ethnic heritage, carried a sadness and a longing for a life that would allow her to experience love and excitement not found in her arranged marriage as the wife of an inn manager. She had two children, first a girl, insufficient to provide her status in the marriage. Her son, born four years later, gave her power bestowed by the negotiations for her second pregnancy, giving her more influence and authority. She, affectionately referred to as Her Laziness, now controlled the amount of work she performed, the money she was permitted to spend, and an elevated position within their community. Nonetheless, while appearing naive and innocent, flaunting her native reticence, she possessed all the same negative qualities as her husband in no less degree. They, together, shared sloth and avarice of monumental proportions.

Their greed originated from the same source: an early life of little luxury and the promise of riches in their new homeland, a promise they intended to fulfill at any cost. In his mind, in addition to all the advantages of technology and money, these new riches included absolute authority over his wife, his children, his parents, his employees, and ultimately the customers who frequented the inn. Those customers furnished him with the opportunity to maintain this new life. The employees, through their expertise, elevated the standards of service and comfort at the inn, affording him a prosperous business.

Their arrogance was more complicated, but explained by cultural and religious influences, psychiatric diagnoses untouchable without a long, protracted course of intense therapy, and an intense desire for change. Their laziness, meanness, and lack of conscience was its own reward. Their difficult personalities insulated them from criticism and confrontation. Disparaging remarks and antagonistic interactions were often dismissed, attributing the individual with stupidity. Tradesmen and customers spent as little time as necessary in their presence. Contractors did their jobs, but most vowed never to return. Any project from start to completion was always an opportunity for him to complain, degrade, annoy, and finally argue over the agreed-upon price. His meanness prevailed, and his rewards were consistent. Wanting to end the obstreperous dialogue, the experienced employees were quick to realize they had no choice but to defer to his terms. These craftsmen took leave with a sigh of relief, happy to have their sanity intact.

Customers ran from the office after a barrage of questions, feeling as though they had been swindled; their assessments were always correct. The inn's patrons were valued according to the make and year of their automobiles. They ranged from important customers to the equivalent of untouchables or "not-nice customers." The untouchables were especially vulnerable. Many had few resources to enter into negotiations from any position of power. Often, they arrived by taxi and had no significant financial resources or emotional support. A room for the night provided the comfort of a hot bath, shelter from harsh weather, and privacy. The rented room, however, did not guarantee seclusion or freedom from harassment. Those who fit in the not-nice category were often subject to his managerial invasion of their personal effects, personal space, and time. An additional charge secreted into the rent was justified to cover any damage they might do. Telephone calls were monitored for time and frequency—and often terminated when their arbitrary time was up. Compassionate concern and respect were never extended to anyone, but his contempt for these patrons was blatantly evident in his intercourse with them. He believed congeniality and respect were unnecessary expenditures of his energy.

Despite his obsequious fawning over the important customers, those patrons were not exempt from his insane treatment. He would enter their rooms in their absence to inspect their luggage, the drawers in which they stored their belongings, and their personal papers. If discovered, he made no excuse and self-righteously stated he was making sure his inn was maintained at his high standard of cleanliness. The rate hikes for these patrons were also camouflaged, not apparent to even the most scrutinizing eye. Although advertised as an AAA-sponsored inn, with promised discounts for members and senior citizens, such discounts did not exist. He asked each prospective patron, before quoting the room's price, if they were subscribers to AAA or above the age of sixty-five. He then priced the room at his standard rate, claiming their discounts were included. Consistent with his mendacity, he inflated the standard rate by the time of day, the desperateness or need of the customers, his evaluation of their financial status, his desire for extra cash, or his own capriciousness.

His day rate, available for those discriminating patrons requiring only a few hours, was conveniently priced at nine-tenths of the original cost. Revenue raked in from this opportunity to rent a room twice in one day made his heart beat faster as he rang up the sale on the register. The lodging business was nearly perfect for his personality. There was, however, an inherent problem. Every morning, he was pained as the cleanup phase approached. The service component of the innkeeper's responsibility was never factored into his workload when he gleefully accepted the customers' credit cards.

In keeping with his binary thinking, he professed the banal belief that to ensure a steady stream of patrons for the inn, the only thing necessary were clean toilet bowls, an obsession he carried to the extreme. When first asked to assist with the cleaning, we were appalled by the abominable conditions of the rooms in general and the bathrooms in particular. After much time and energy, Emily set new standards of cleanliness. This criterion, now incorporated as his own cleaning philosophy, became the new standard. Rooms were now checked against this new norm, and any infraction—legitimate or otherwise—was presented to me on a list to be redone. It was not unusual for a hair to be strategically placed to make his demands seem appropriate. This ridiculous fixation relentlessly continued throughout our time there. It is impossible to know whether he really concerned himself with this absurdity or if it was simply an attempt to assert his imaginary power and conquer the anxiety secondary to the psychiatric diagnosis that overwhelmed him.

The basic component of any psychological deviation is anxiety. To maintain some semblance of emotional equilibrium, this anxiety must be assuaged. There are several avenues through which this angst may be quelled: prescribed psychotropic drugs, behavioral modification, and/or intense psychotherapy. All these interventions require a level of self-consciousness usually missing in psychologically impaired minds. More commonly, anxiety is handled by self-medication—alcohol, illegal drugs, illicitly obtained psychopharmacological prescriptions—or displacement, where the psyche seeks an alternative avenue of expression to subsume the recurrent anxiety. For example, anger is externalized toward those individuals who the person believes is responsible for their anxiety. Their total lack of self-understanding necessitated the latter approach for defusing their panic. They extravagantly displayed anger and retaliation as displacement mechanisms. Their true madness was seen in the extensive and unrealistic levies they placed on patrons and employees while remaining incapable and insensitive to those same demands for themselves.

Much of their thought processes may be traced to their cultural and religious heritage. While politically and legally nonexistent, the ancient custom of dividing whole groups of peoples into an impermeable caste system still exists in the consciousness of many Indian immigrants, particularly those moving from rural villages. With perfected mental gymnastics, this couple justified the immoral treatment of family members, acquaintances, employees, and customers by placing them in an imaginary status lower than their own—in spite of experiencing indoor plumbing for the first time as a result of recently immigrating to the United States.

Their perpetuation of this mythical status system became one avenue through which their collective anxieties could be alleviated. Much of the acting out toward the inn patrons and their menials was the result of the irrational fears they projected onto those individuals. Any inadequacy they felt was remedied by placing those people within a status inferior to themselves. The manager and his wife became easily angered and retaliatory against those they feared. They projected this fear by showing total disregard and even delight for the human misfortune and misery they evidenced in those poor folks who were unfortunate enough to be homeless or desperate for any variety of reasons.

Jesus pleased his audience in a simple parable:

> He said, "Two men went up to the temple to pray ...
> The one prayed, 'God, I thank thee that I am not as
> other men (he then enumerated at length the evils he
> did not do and the good things he believed he did do).
> The other, standing afar off, did not even so much as
> lift up his head, but, smiting his breast, said, 'God be
> merciful to me a sinner.' I tell you this man went down
> to his house justified ... Everyone who exalts himself will
> be abased; but he that humbles himself will be exalted."
> (Luke 18:9–14)

Humility, because of their anxiety, could not be incorporated into their personalities. He refused to accept checks from sponsoring charitable organizations and local churches. Higher rates were charged for the rooms he permitted to be rented to these unfortunate souls. Harassing them unmercifully, he would shut off their phone service even for incoming calls, and they were forced to leave their rooms during cleanings. Relentlessly, he inquired how soon they would be checking out while receiving cash payments in excess of the norm. As an innkeeper, he recreated the Christmas story each day.

Witnessing any kindness, he would say, "Why are you so nice? Why do you care?"

I said, "It is the right thing to do. People should be treated with respect and care."

His face scrunched with confusion, he would simply declare, "We can't do that here. That's not the way we do this business."

The religious milieu within which the manager and his wife lived for the majority of their lives was intensely individualistic. The various competing theologies of Buddhism, Hinduism, and Confucianism place great merit on individual toil and satisfaction as the avenues to Karmic enlightenment. In Hinduism and Buddhism particularly, Karma is most important. It is the consequences of a person's actions during the several successive phases of reincarnation that determine the soul's destiny. (Kr, in Sanskrit deriving from *karoti*, a verbal form from which the nominative *karron*—Hindi: *karma*—is derived, designates an action of the soul.)

The Hindu understanding of karma lacks any altruistic outreach and is isolationist. In Buddhist thinking, the acts—and the consequences of those acts—attach directly and only to the individual and are not corporate activities. It is more important for the person to do good within the Buddhist theological structure for himself than to do good for those individuals who surround him. Nonhuman species (mice, rats, monkeys, and cattle) are cared for and respected far above other humans. In a common picture from India's teeming cities, a Brahman bull decked with flowers walks serenely past a recumbent beggar; the lice infecting his skin and clothing are of more value than the soul of this child of God. Such attitudes contrast sharply with the altruism preached as moral conduct by Western Judeo-Christian religions.

In the only parable Jesus ever used regarding entrance into the Kingdom of God (Matthew 25:31–46), Jesus enunciated the Christian principle of altruism. Acceptance into heaven is based upon our care of and our relationship with others. The principle is simple: whatever you do for others, you do for God. The opposite (immorality) is concomitantly true: that which you do not do for others, you do not do for God. Doing equates to acceptability into the kingdom of God; conversely, not doing is unacceptable. Noncaring isolationism is, in Christian theology, reprehensible.

To this couple, such altruism was completely foreign. The combination of psychiatric maladaptations—narcissistic socio-pathology and passive-aggressive motivational impulsivity—coupled with a preexisting social system of hierarchy and a Theo-philosophical disregard for any human condition other than their own, paved the way for the enticement of my ex-wife to become their evil companion.

Both of these identifications—narcissism and passive-aggressive personality—might need some clarification. The first derives from the Greek myth of Narcissus, a youth who, spurning the love of Echo became enamored with the reflection of his own visage in a quiet pool of water. The consequence of his obsession was that he was to be frozen forever in the form of the flower that bears his name. In psychological terminology, narcissism is an obsessive-compulsive fixation on the superiority of one's self. In the psychotherapeutic understanding of this malady, it is the regression of the individual into an infantile state and the erotic self-pleasure therein derived. Against this aberration, Saint Paul, in his letter to the Roman Church, advises, "Do not think of yourself more highly than you ought" (Romans 12:3).

The passive-aggressive personality identifies a psychological displacement in which the individual, disturbed by the circumstances that surround him or the opinions people hold of him, reacts with a calmed projection followed inappropriately by intense anger and retribution. This ignores the Hebrew-Christian theological injunction, "Vengeance is mine says the Lord, I will repay them" (Romans 12:19). This disorder attempts at some later date to demand the revenge the psyche believes it needs.

The etiology of an individual's descent into insane evil is as follows:

- rationalizing what one has done, rather than reasoning what one should do
- holding obsessively to beliefs and customs for which there is no longer external verification

- condemning one's conscience (that inner moral voice) as an irrelevant appendage from an archaic Judeo-Christian past, totally out of step with our modern, more fluid, moral "correctness" and culture
- isolating one's self and progeny ("after all, they must choose for themselves") from both the private and public practice of any specific religion
- succumbing to an attraction (sometimes reaching obsession and preoccupation) to the accoutrement of evil: "good people" wishing to identify with biker clubs or street gangs by their dress and speech, subsequently becoming enamored with the violence, death, and destruction on television, at automobile races, or in professional sports contests
- using the good (God) to enjoy the world rather than using the world to enjoy or promote "the good"

Any of these, separately or together, exacerbates the psychological and psychiatric character defects that accelerate an individual's fall into the absolute darkness of moral reprobation. The insidious decline is not unlike a man standing at the equator, unconscious that he and the world beneath his feet are rotating at approximately a thousand miles an hour. With the gravitational and centrifugal forces equaled, he feels no movement. For that man at the equator, with no external point of reference in the universe possesses nothing by which to gauge his movement, like sitting in an airplane in a cloudless sky traveling at five hundred miles an hour, no apparent sense of motion exists. With no point of departure or desire to seek models of moral behavior, they found it impossible to judge the increasing speed of their darkening evil.

Concurrent with starting a project requiring an extended time commitment, extended family meetings were arranged. Reportedly, these get-togethers provided an opportunity for several inn owners and managers to share ideas and business strategies. Previously unable to find an honest and capable employee to manage the inn in his absence, they had never before been able to participate. He asked if I would tend the office since I was already on the premises working on another project. I was not flattered. My honesty was merely another reason to exploit me for his

11

selfish purposes. This was one among our many topics of conflict and discord.

In contrast to his own deceitfulness, he presented monumental paranoia. He depended on his ability to get them before they get you. His personality structure demanded he believe that what he would do to others, they, of course, would do to him. He obsessively concerned himself with the safety of his property, refusing to leave any article in the rooms or on the grounds unbolted. Initially, the inn's televisions were on small, moveable floor stands, available to even a most inept thief. To date, no TV had been stolen, nevertheless, to discharge his apprehension, he asked me to fashion locking wall mounts upon which the sets could be securely positioned. From metal, I cut, formed, and welded thirty-one such fixtures. Now, to his satisfaction, the requisite security had been achieved. With his self-serving mantra, and his projection that everyone lives by the same trickery, prevarication, and negative judgments as he, it is not surprising that his paranoia knew no limits. His fears and distrust extended into the most obscure corners of his character.

The family's absences at first were confined to a single day, but they soon were extended to several days—sometimes even as long as two weeks. We were not necessarily informed on departure how long they would be gone. They simply said they would telephone us to give their arrival time. He resisted my demands to know his destination and telephone number. Indeed, he admonished that if someone should call for him, we were to say, "I am temporarily out of the office," and to offer no further information. When asked what we should do in an emergency, he told me that I knew how to handle any emergency and that he would call me in those instances. He would check in with me by phone daily. The owner of the inn was not to be called under any circumstances. Likewise, no one was to be told he was away or where he could be reached. What was he hiding? Had his paranoid delusions any basis in fact—or were they simply the projections of a mind that had already rationalized its own incursions beyond the boundaries of the self into the psychic domains of others?

In contemporary psychological terminology, this is quite often identified as a borderline personality disorder. The symptoms include generalized, as well as specific, paranoiac ideation, self-destructive tendencies based on that ideation, an inability to form relationships, a difficulty in communication, and an inability to distinguish personal boundaries. All these, to some extent, he exhibited.

It was evident there was a peculiar strangeness about this family, the organization of the corporation, and its economic stability. Although constantly professing poverty secondary to low customer interest and income, there were always monies for materials necessary for the large renovation projects. He purchased, to name a few, roof shingles, vinyl siding, floor tiles, windows, twenty-seven-inch televisions and air conditioners for all the units, and a plethora of toys for himself. And, while claiming such poverty, he excused himself from the obligation of financial remuneration for the additional services I was performing, constantly reminding me, as first discussed, that these additional monies would be available to me upon my departure from the inn. His reluctance to pay me can be partially explained by his borderline symptomatology. There was, in his mind, little distinction between him and me, between what he needed and what I could provide. It was as though he and I were identical. This incorporation of one personality (external) by the experiencing personality into its own (internalization) was a trait both he and the Angel of Death shared in common.

We believed, as did several other perspicacious patrons and local businessmen, that something was very economically questionable, immoral, and/or illegal at the inn and in every corner of the economic negotiations and purviews. Money was always available for his own projects and his own "toys." From whence these additional finances came was conjectured, debated, anecdotalized, and mythologized. There were no firm answers, only suspicions. One answer to this conundrum was the Angel of Death herself. Was she the silent backer or banker in return for which our incarceration at the inn was paramount? Was his reluctance to pay me refusal? Did his greed and immorality win? Did a lack of conscience permit them to perpetuate the myth that kept us enveloped in their evil malignancy? How did the Angel of Death recognize a mirroring of her own mean evilness to feel secure that this couple would participate in her malicious and illegal scheme? Or was it something beyond what we could imagine or wrap our minds around?

Chapter 2

The Inheritance

EMILY AND I are both highly educated. While working with my hands as a blacksmith like my grandfather and a roofer like my father was my preference, the ridiculous struggle to be paid and the insatiable expectations quickly became a stress that I could no longer tolerate. However, darkening clouds were looming on our personal horizons. Our decisions, we would later discover, would not be our own for a very long time.

One sunny afternoon, I received a substantial gift from my grandmother. Unfamiliar with the financial world, I turned my inheritance over to my accountant: the man I trusted for many years to do my taxes, the man I could and did call for advice on money matters. As a management fee, he received 5 percent of the portfolio proceeds. I genuinely liked him, and it seemed that this generous percentage would be a deterrent to theft or mismanagement. I left the gift in his capable hands and was consistently satisfied with his performance. The inheritance grew at a steady rate.

In addition to his CPA's code of professional ethics, he was instructed to strictly adhere to the rules of confidentiality, never to discuss my grandmother's estate with anyone, most especially my then-wife, the Angel of Death. For several years, the relationship between us had been deteriorating. Infidelity, consistent misuse of my funds, and a pregnancy conceived that was not my own set the stage for our contractual dissolution. My injunction to my accountant, that nothing of this inheritance be revealed to her, was monumentally important. I feared the loss of my bequest or my life or both. These feelings, as events would shortly reveal, were not paranoid.

Two years before this adventure at the inn, during an unexpected encounter, a shocked old friend blurted, "I thought you were dead!"

Pursuing this absurdity, I discovered, that, indeed, everyone who knew me had been told I was dead. With the collusion of my accountant, she achieved initial success, giving her the impetus to continue down this road. The taxes were paid on my fortune and transferred to an abandoned account just waiting for the day it could be claimed by her. She had wound her black-taloned tentacles around my friend, compelling him to consent to her dark charade. What had she promised? What secret did he not want her to reveal? What was so frightening that he would betray me and surrender such a large commission and face criminal charges should he be caught?

In the courts, my life was ended. She had me declared dead, based on her testimony that I could not be found. With most of my income and savings needed for the necessary care of the physical and financial needs of my ill parents, there was little left for a lawyer to assist me with my resurrection. Acting as my own attorney, I depended on those familiar with the process to provide me with the appropriate forms and procedures for filing and scheduling court dates. With assistance and cooperation from the court employees, the procedures went smoothly. However, a judgment never meant resolution in spite of the court's promises. At the time of my parents' deaths, the legal battle had not yet been won.

While Emily and I took care of my ill parents, we examined the legal intricacies surrounding my death. Progress, if there were any at all, was measured at a snail's pace. Inexplicably, my portfolio was still out of my reach, despite my "being alive." Explanations for the enigma ranged from pure ineptness to the lack of sophisticated equipment; they were a small and poorly funded legal system. These excuses remained unchanged regardless of where I poked for information or answers.

My money and the requisite help needed to finally steal my fortune were the objects of her obsession and the vehicle with which she would torture me for the remainder of my life.

With consistent optimism for resolution, we worked as we were led to think, with our bank's president. He was an imposing figure, a full head of silver hair and a smile offering confidence in his professional authority. We met within weeks of our move to discuss the transfer of my inheritance and to set up a charitable trust. He showed to me, on his computer screen, pertinent information referencing the funds to be transferred from the abandoned account. Given the intricacies of my financial difficulties, my banker suggested I retain an attorney to assist me and advise me in the handling of my inheritance and those responsible for its disappearance. This reputable attorney—without any face-to-face contact and referred by the bank—agreed to represent us. His deep voice and command of the legal intricacies necessary for successful adjudication of our problems gave me a sense of safety and hope. He reported his association with the bank was assurance enough that he would be paid when the matter was settled; he also was purposing that, in the future, we could discuss the possibility of his assuming executorship of my estate.

I was confident that our conversation was genuine; after all, the president was sitting at his desk, in his office, in his bank. It seemed, at last, there was an avenue for resolution. I was excited and feeling hopeful, resigned to tolerate the inanities of the inn since our time there was limited. I was, after all, a very wealthy man with an obscene inheritance that I was sure I could enjoy. Emily and I planned our travel itineraries, the home we would purchase in Scotland or Italy, and the joy of sharing this money through charitable gifts.

Emily and I love each other, and our time together is easy and fun no matter what we are doing. We made the most of what we believed was a temporary situation by looking forward to being free of this madness once again. Daily, we were promised that these difficulties would be resolved— sometimes within a month and sometimes within a week. We were often encouraged to wait day by day, but there were always excuses why they— the banker and the attorney—could not accomplish these tasks. In our ignorance, we continued to put our trust and faith in the process into which we were led, the good faith agreement with the inn's manager, and the pursuit of my inheritance. We would, however, find that nothing in our lives was private, real, or done in good faith.

Chapter 3

The Angel of Death

F ORTY YEARS AGO, I met a bright, educated, and vibrant woman introduced to me by a friend; a blind date brought two people together with the same interests. Among the many languages I commanded was French; she, fluent in French, was a student of that rich culture. We met at an art gallery. Our conversation was easy, with long, interesting discussions of history, art, poetry, and the myriad interests we shared. I was excited to think that, after recently ending a long and extremely painful relationship, there could be fun and love again. It wasn't long before we were spending most of our days and nights together. We belonged to an exclusive club and ate at wonderful restaurants. Employment at prestigious universities afforded us opportunities for a fascinating social life. Caught up in all the good, the insidiousness of her progressing mental illness was overlooked, completely missed.

What was admired as an ability to make friends easily was later recognized as an inability to maintain her emotional boundaries. The thrill of her wanting my company turned to apprehension as her possessiveness, stemming from her inability to be alone with herself, took over. A child not nurtured, unable to trust the world, obsessively seeks comfort and panics when the object of that comfort (whomever it may be at that moment) is unavailable either emotionally or from physical distance. She was self-abusive and had a history of addictive behaviors.

A victim of psychological abuse by a mother with a protracted bipolar disorder, she remained attached to her victimization through her own emerging borderline personality disorder. Somewhere in her developing mental illness, she also lost her conscience. She had become a diagnosable sociopath.

As a child matures, the psyche seeks to provide for its wants and needs in some kind of a protective environment. That environment usually is the family. If the child finds the security he or she needs along with understanding within that safety of the family, these demands can be met. The child learns stability, develops a conscience, and learns the necessity of postponing certain gratifications. If such a secure encompassment is absent, the infantile needs, together with infantile avenues for obtaining it, are perpetuated long into adolescence and young adulthood. Without amelioration of the threatening emotional atmosphere, needs become paramount, conscience dulls, and personal boundaries disappear. True socio-pathology results. Like the psychotic narcissist, the sociopath perpetuates the infantilization of everything about them: only their desires matter, only their needs should be met, and the only guilt is that which other personalities must bear for the difficulties experienced by the true sociopath.

The narcissistic sociopath (the exacerbation of a borderline diagnosis) is a truly seductive malady for both lay and professional persons alike. Their propensities for self-destruction—suicidal ideation (more manipulative than actual threat), willing acceptance of the victimization role, monumental self-pity, and insatiable need—seduce any individuals who possess consciousness or caring thoughts. The continued association of other personalities with the sociopath is demanded by the manipulative and seductive victimization that the socio-pathological personality projects.

The self-destructive activities and suicidal attempts of individuals accompanied by psychotic psychiatric diagnoses are, at the beginning, demands for attention or cries for help. The intention is not death but recognition. The classic illustration is a wife waking her husband, showing him an empty bottle of pills, and saying, "See what I did?"

Persons with true suicidal intent execute their plans in isolation and in silence so there is no possibility of interference. In socio-pathology and borderline psychiatrically diagnosed personalities, self-inflicted cutting or the self-ingested overdose of medications are means by which these individuals garner recognition and sympathy. As the families, psychiatric systems, and helping agencies become inured to their client's recurrent suicidal threats and feeble posturing (much like the boy who cried wolf), the afflicted individuals must increase the severity of their "death-inviting" attempts. Most of these individuals who eventually succeed do so by accident rather than intent; they ingest more than they had planned, miscalculate their ability to obtain help, or erroneously anticipate their threats will be taken seriously.

I was honest and monogamous, busy with my work and what I believed was a happy union. My mind never entertained what was really the truth of my life. After our marriage, the degeneration was more rapid. Suicidal ideation and threats became the norm for the day. I became the psychologist instead of the husband. The anger directed at me forced confrontations that eventuated in my leaving, time and again.

A phone call during one of the separations brought an unwelcome pronouncement. She was pregnant. My vasectomy was ten years old. "If you leave me, I'll have an abortion," she cried. My ethical system left no room for such an affront to this unborn child. She hoped just such a threat would ensure my maintaining the facade of a family. I needed time to consider all the ramifications of my decision, but while I was thinking, her alcohol consumption increased, further threatening this unborn child. We reconciled with the understanding the marriage would be ended should she ever tell our daughter I was not her father.

Despite not sharing a connubial bed, there was a period of peace while we cleared the land and I began to build a home, a dream I had since my youth. My blacksmith shop flourished, as did our daughter. My daughter consumed my heart; my decision to be her father felt so right. I adored her, and she adored me. For ten years, I shared her days, the good and the bad. The good allowed her bright, inquisitive nature to probe and extract the contents of my mind through endless questions and pronouncements. Her creativity demanded elaborate stories that I made up, monopolizing much of our evenings together. Each bedtime, our itinerary would include three different made-up tales and the *Wizard of Oz*. She would drift off to sleep during Dorothy's adventures, but the words and their sequence must always be exactly the same. Should I skip a word or change the inflection of my voice, she would awaken and remind me of the mistake, then return to her reverie. Her unspoken hopes and fears found voice and expression when she nightly wrote to the mythical characters we made up. Each morning, she would find the answers in a mythical mailbox that would comfort her and start her day on an even course.

Our flock of sheep promoted an avenue for many of life's teachings: witnessing the birth of a precious lamb and understanding sadness and loss by the death of a four-legged companion. Instinctively, she grasped my passion for the forge, sharing many an afternoon helping and creating original pieces of her own. She was truly my daughter.

Protecting her from the bad came to be overwhelmingly necessary. Her mother's character disorder left no room for tolerating the loving bond that formed between my daughter and me. Jealous of my affection, angered by our shared interests and time, and enraged by the trust that provided her safety, her mother lashed out at both of us. Unpredictable, the timing and expression of her outbursts left no room for preparation. The physical abuse attempted toward this child was always thwarted by my intervention: removing her mother or physically moving between them always culminated in the abuse being leveled against me. Protecting her from her mother's emotional and psychological harassment demanded intense and more sophisticated interventions. Not a few times, with knife in hand, did this disordered woman scream, "I'm going to kill myself. You will find my body in the morning." Begging and crying, my daughter would hold on to me as she watched the raging figure leave through the front door. Constantly reminding her that her mother's threats were not real—coupled with the comfort and familiarity of our nightly story ritual—my frightened child would fall asleep in my arms, hoping for a new day that would bring back a saner, more reasonable maternal being.

In a fit of anger, these words were spoken: "He is not your father."

Freud once said that sometimes a cigar, rather than some deep psychiatric symbol, was just a good smoke. We might analyze her socio-pathological need to reveal the forbidden, but her jealousy won out. It was the ultimate betrayal. She refused to accept a separation and denied me parental access, pronouncing my daughter was not mine. After some intense negotiations, I agreed to move into a hotel for a weekend while she ostensibly was removing her belongings from my house. She consented. I would have custody, and she would enjoy liberal visitation and access to my house in my absence. I was not intent on revenge; I only wanted quiet sanity for my daughter and me. This hopeful trust and critical mistake cost me my daughter, my home, and my peace.

The most was made of this indignation; she claimed ownership of my house based on abandonment of the property. Legally she removed my surname from my daughter's birth certificate. Daily, hourly, I attempted contact. Sent gifts never found their way into her hands or her heart. She didn't know how my heart ached, how my silenced stories screamed to reach her ears, how communicating through our mythical characters would connect us and ease the sadness. I could only pray that the nine years of careful nurturing and memories of my commitment and love would sustain her and give her strength. Impotent, I was unable to change her plight either physically or legally; she was not my child. I was counseled that legally I had no rights with my daughter—and any interference would only result in legal action against me.

Paternity was, however, not a determinant in the court's decision to award child support, nor was the hypocrisy of no visitation because I was not the biological father. Fraudulent financial statements, not revealing her substantial assets, were never brought into question. The theft of my tools, which limited my ability to make a living, and the illegal acquisition of my home were never addressed. Yet another way was found to make my life more miserable.

I miss my daughter. My soul aches with her absence.

Chapter 4

Planning for the Future with Excitement

OUR PRIVACY IS most prized. Emily and I are a self-contained, sustainable unit. There are few things short of services from a medical doctor that we could not do for ourselves. There is nothing I cannot fix from cars to machinery; my wife's sewing and knitting skills can make a fifty-cent rummage sale garment into a designer's dream. Artistically, we share the same vision. We are the other's biggest fan and toughest critic. The dolls she creates are dressed with fabric draped over frames I construct from discarded wood. Recycled objects force creativity and imagination with the materials dictating the vision.

Professionally, our backgrounds are similar. As a psychologist and she a therapist, we understand each other and the workings of the human psyche. Working together is as smooth as a well-oiled machine. We always seem to know what part to play in the process. We make an effective, efficient team and are able to accomplish most tasks in record time, at minimal cost, and with the highest quality. And so it was at the inn, which provided more than enough opportunities for our skills to be practiced.

Emily knew nothing of construction, but she learned quickly and made every new construction project move along with ease. With the precision of an OR scrub nurse, the correct tool was in my hand, the necessary materials were available as they were needed, and the area was swept to prevent accidents and avoid additional time at the end of the day for cleanup. We kept to ourselves, completed our contracted work, and pursued every opportunity to extricate our persons from that untenable situation.

Within a few months, the outward appearance of the inn looked drastically different. New windows, vinyl siding, and fresh paint brought the praise of patrons and townsfolk. Frequent business with local suppliers brought friendships and conversation. The discussion often got around to the manager. When discussing the manager's reputation, sentences were peppered with words like *mean, nasty, hateful, cheap, unscrupulous, criminal,* and *arrogant.* The list was essentially an incessant litany of negative descriptive adjectives characterizing the various interactions and transactions between them. He never paid his bills on time, if at all; he was rude and derogatory on the phone and mercilessly blamed the merchants for late or damaged merchandise. It was dependent on my intercession and friendships with business owners and managers to smooth the way for him to get the best deal and additional services. His hatefulness infected everyone he touched, leaving me to restore order and communication.

I was exhausted from the work and the psychological strain. Each interaction was a therapeutic intervention that demanded my constant attention. Our life was losing momentum, and each day was frustrated with new difficulties. Emily could not understand why two talented, educated individuals could find themselves in this situation. All we wanted was a home, a place to create, and most of all, to be left alone. All of which were imminently within our grasp given my inheritance, our education, and our talents. The stress was keeping me in physical and emotional pain. My legs ached, my stomach was always upset, and my sleep was fretful. Finding a way to expedite the release of my inheritance became my top priority; conversely, implementing new and creative ways of keeping my fortune hidden was my ex-wife's goal.

Entering into the mix of my death, the promises of the lawyer and banker, and the day-to-day misery imposed was the voice. The phone rang, starting the day after we arrived at the inn. The voice—sometimes male, sometimes female—brought a message on an average of every two weeks. The message was a threat to Emily's life, a life that would be spared with my cooperation. The awesome responsibility for her safety lay in my hands. For my continued work at the inn and my silence about these calls, her life would be of no interest to the initiator of these threats. I was instructed not to call the police, a private investigator, a newspaper reporter, or even a friend. I carried this secret alone, all the while watching my wife sink further into her frustration and unhappiness. My heart broke a little more with each tear she shed.

The seriousness of those dark threats must be seen from the absoluteness of the unconditional love that Emily and I share. We spent twenty-four hours a day together and enjoyed each moment. Our similar and not-so-similar interests gave us more than enough topics about which to talk. My greatest joy is waking each morning to see her face and knowing her love surrounds me. My greatest fear was a successful execution of the threats to her life. I could not face my life without her. I realized I was the only one who could protect her—and I would. Some years ago, while we were physically separated, I wrote the following poem for her:

Purple, blue-hued,
Velvet scented reams,
Surround me now
Across unencumbered horizons;
Softness and light,
Pink and blue ambered clouds
Float wraithlike,
Dissolving the hardness
Of my unextended cold, reality;
They tell me that this must be real,
What snobbery that they think they know,
And, in their thinking,
To believe they held my spirit *prisoned*,
Like a moth, trapped
In a seventh-grade science project.
Where Icarus failed to fly,
There I can freely soar;
Resting on the enfolding fire
Of your love,
The sweetness of your mystic presence,
The constancy of your psychic touch;
These, these be my realities,
You, my life.

I felt helpless. Keeping a secret from Emily was antithetical to the promise we had made to each other. Trust is the foundation of our relationship, and I was betraying that trust, reconciled only by the belief that her life was more important. The voice on the phone made it clear her life was in more danger if she were not always within the sound of my voice. I couldn't tell her I would have done anything short of jeopardizing her safety to leave this atrocious situation.

There were no explanations I could offer Emily, but the answer finally appeared in the form of two men in black cars with multiple antennas flashing badges that identified them as FBI. The FBI agents, the banker, and the attorney became daily telephone voices (plural, to distinguish them from the voice that was leveling the threats). These agents confirmed the reports: my Emily was in danger. They, however, were assigned to protect her. Their presence would be in the background; no one would know they were shadowing, but she would never be out of their sight. The malicious game spun out of control, especially out of our control. This was a revengeful, desperate woman with an impossible, illegal, and dangerous plan.

She intended to gain control of a fortune worth millions without detection. She was using, with success, the state's child-support division. Her focused, task-oriented energy was consistently rewarded. She was, after all, brilliant, economically savvy, and unconscionably ruthless. This obsessive pursuit was her retribution for the imaginary abandonment by the husband, the psychologist, the caretaker, and the father of her child. Her rage like her boundaryless personality had no check. She was humiliated, furious, and frightened. I was going to pay with everything I had—even my life and Emily's life if necessary.

Chapter 5

Identity Theft

MY EX-WIFE WAS among those in a long list of ancestral lineage, most of whom were Congregational clergymen and theologians. She was well versed in the history, literature, and polity of that branch of the Christian Church. Theologically, she was a Calvinist (everything that one does is predetermined by the Deity) which, radically construed, is a fine handmaiden for socio-pathology (nothing one does is either their fault or their responsibility). In the two sinister hands of a warped psychology and a truncated theology, the Angel of Death was more than capable, more than exhilarated, at the murderous schemes she was beginning to weave successfully about our lives. This demon was excited by the prospects of her damnable plots, and she felt that she had been divinely ordered to execute them. Much in ancient literature (particularly Egyptian and Hellenic) speaks of female psyches twisted by homophobic paranoia into degenerate spirits intent on revenge.

One need only mention Medusa, where one glance from her turned males to stone. In Homer's *Iliad*, we read the graphic description of the Argonauts' tragic experiences: the Sirenic songs causing them to row their ships upon the rocks. Only Jason roped to the mast, eyes and ears bound, was able to stay his course, and the fabled Queen Hatshepsut, by whose assassinations and military coups established herself both queen and pharaoh. These angry women are her historical and literary archetypes. In contemporary films such as *She-Devil* and *Waiting to Exhale*, we see and even applaud the female protagonists as they systematically go about destroying the personal and financial lives of the men to whom their anger is turned—even to the point of stripping them of their freedom. If, as Goethe reminds us in Faust, a soul may sell itself to the demonic forces of Satan, then the power derived from this contract is all but infinite. Such a contractual arrangement seems to have been made by her whom we have identified as the Angel of Death.

Through her angry machinations, the vortex continued to swirl about us. Much within her plots seemed plausible to us, fitting in with what we knew of bureaucracy and the legal system. What we were told by telephone, confirmed by "legal documents" provided by the friendly FBI agents and the inn manager's authentications, we now know reflected her plotting, outlandish and implausible. The plots were so bizarre that we believed they must be true; surely no one could have made up such impossible situations.

Because of the crescendo of mounting threats, the FBI assigned a special agent, with whom we could speak at any time. She proved herself available to us, calling at various times of the day or night to assure us of our safety. She would communicate the ways the FBI was protecting us. Over the course of several months, my ex-wife's Mephistophelian incursions included twelve different scenarios of who was stalking us with intent to harm.

In anticipation of receiving the inheritance, my father, Emily, and I spent the day with a Realtor looking for a house. Our plans for a home together took us to a small Realtor with a friendly shingle hanging above the door. The broker was personable with a sense of humor not unlike my own. I knew that long hours in the car traveling from property to property would be an enjoyable time. After a few days, we found just that house, but it was tied to the settling of my grandmother's estate.

The house stood stately and elegant with a three-story detached barn from which I could imagine a workshop like no other. Exploring the interior of the house was a mere formality. This was to be our home. Sporting several bedrooms, an enormous living room, and a kitchen engulfed in delicious smells, we could envision this house full of family and friends. In the quaint sitting room, images of my reading, Emily knitting, and Dad sleeping comfortably in front of the fire solidified our dream. Dad picked out his bedroom; Emily emerged from the windowed porch and proclaimed, "We must have this house." We returned home tired and satisfied that Grandma's generosity to me was a gift I treasured as much as the memories of the love I evidenced every day, especially when she placed a huge bowl of lemon pudding (ostensibly, leftover from the pie she was making) at my place at the table. Our excited decision would soon turn to yet another opportunity to manipulate our lives.

Dad was the youngest of four sons. The eldest was twenty years older than my dad. He had little memory of his older brother who left home at a very young age. Grandma's middle two sons were close in age to each other but still ten years older than my father. Both sons died suddenly in accidents just months apart. My grandmother never really recovered, but at my birth, she found a reason for joy and a reason to give thanks to God. I delighted in the love I shared with her. My grandfather, a blacksmith, surrounded me with love and imparted to me the greatest gift to my soul. He filled my life with the wonder of fire and metal, a new expression of creativity, a new way of meditating, a new way to connect with my God.

Dad was my best friend, my first fan. He and my mother encouraged and applauded my every effort. I excelled academically and athletically. Football, the sport my father played, gave us many enjoyable days playing, watching, or just discussing my high school and college games, his high school career, or the antics of all the other college and professional teams. In fact, the last words before he died were, "Is football on tonight?"

Music connected us too. Dad loved the violin, which he played with great skill until rheumatoid arthritis twisted his digits into painful knots. And he also loved the opera. I can easily, hearing the voice of a tenor, be transported to a Saturday afternoon watching the ecstasy fill the face of this extraordinary man as the songs of Mario Lanza or Enrico Caruso glided from the radio. Sharing the great things in our life provided openings to talk about the difficulties. We guided each other through myriad problems, knowing that whatever was said was accepted unconditionally. My father's wisdom was prized above all. We all wanted—needed—him with us. His health was failing, his wife of seventy-two years no longer knew him, and he needed the safety, love, and caring Emily and I wanted to give. They said Dad died of congestive heart failure, but really, his heart was broken. I miss him, especially in the mornings when we would share coffee, questions about most anything, or just the silence that enveloped our love for each other. The house and my father were added to the list of ideas with which I could be tortured. It was a work in progress. There was much to do and much more fun to be had.

Many years after our separation and filing for divorce, it came to my attention that my ex-wife had been married very young and then separated from her husband after only a few weeks. Since they hadn't established a home together, no divorce was ever obtained. The rules and laws both natural and man-made did not apply to her. Her exemptions were divinely bestowed, and subsequently, no consequences could ever befall her. She believed she had total immunity from any consequences resulting from her actions. This lack of concern for personal negative outcomes follows directly from her Calvinist theology and a psychological diagnosis of socio-pathology. She felt total freedom to plot and act against anyone threatening her psychological triad: borderline personality disorder, passive-aggressive personality disorder, and socio-pathology (I, my, mine, me). What's mine is mine—and what's yours is mine. The cliché was the maxim by which she lived. She saw no psychic separation between her and me. My leaving stripped her of any external brakes or control, an external superego. If Emily was an obstacle to her possessing me, she felt that Emily must be incorporated into her boundaryless personality and then eliminated (literally) as a nonessential part of that personality. Knowing this, my fears concerning Emily's safety were not unfounded.

None of her actions were fraught with adverse consequences, and such negative outcomes should not be inferred by anyone. She felt at total liberty, without external restrictions, to think or do whatever her evil, calculating mind envisioned. Her actions troubled all about her and did not bother her; any bother was someone else's responsibility. Her psyche knew no boundaries, her actions without limitations. She was like a forest fire fanned by hurricane winds, consuming everything within its path with no conscience or regrets.

She reacted to opposition particularly fiercely when she discovered her own deficiencies in that opposition. They must pay since it was their fault she and they acted out these personality inadequacies together. The following poem I wrote many years ago outlines this psychological process.

"He died," Hemlock breathed,
"Because he dared the question;
And exposed a dreaded hiddenness."
He meant no disrespect,

No challenge to their deepest faiths and suppositions;
He asked of them only clarification;
But their fears, entrenched,
Drove them to assassinate
Their own worst selves
In their philosophical friend,
So, each kills that which he fears
When it becomes manifest,
For we fear nothing quite so much
As the inadequacies we know we possess;
And not even these foibles half so much
As the shame of their discovery
In someone else.

So, her tornadic passions swept onward, around, and through our lives. Her intent was to wound, destroy, and incapacitate us—and thwart all our attempts at extrication. To all this, we would only later become fully aware.

Chapter 6

Disintegration of Family Relationships

I N THE PROCESS of living through our days at the inn, we were barely cognizant of the immensity of forces, bureaucracies, and financial and legal entanglements being placed about us. We would discover bank accounts, lines of credit, and credit cards were obtained in our names using personal information she had stolen from us. The mailing address for these financial transactions was a post office box registered in our name but not known to us. Credit card bills were unpaid, and loans went unsatisfied.

With the advent of affordable computer scanners, internet access to personal information, and the intoxicating draw of acquiring possessions without payment obligation, identity theft is one of the most pervasive crimes of our time, growing exponentially every year. My ex-wife's motivation extended far beyond any thrill of free merchandise. In fact, the theft was only a means to the end: the acquisition of my inheritance and the elimination of Emily. With a powerful computer—purchased with money from Emily's bank account—and her expert computer skills, she had the mechanical and creative means to recreate official documents, checks, and birth and death certificates. At the same time, through internet access, she possessed the ability to obtain crucial personal information about whomever she wished through social security and driver's license numbers, genealogical information, and bank account access numbers—indeed, anything in the public record. With these capabilities, she invaded our lives like a virus that infects, controls, and interrupts an unprotected computer system. She created an impenetrable atmosphere that encapsulated Emily and me. The only information that moved in and out of our world was that which she controlled.

Emily's financial interests were in the hands of our accountant, done at the beginning of our marriage. Her assets included a still-mortgaged condominium she rented and a significant savings account. It was agreed he would collect the rent from the tenants, pay the mortgage, and invest the savings with the same acumen my portfolio had been handled. Periodic communication assured me her money was secure, the condo was in good repair, and the tenants were content. These, of course, were lies. The collusion between my accountant and my ex-wife, whether consensual or coerced, eventuated in the selling of Emily's property at auction. The mortgage not paid, the house was bought in foreclosure and resold for their profit. Stealing Emily's identity and devastating her economically was fun, easy, and rewarding.

Emily's money and the ruination of her credit rating were not, however, sufficient acquisitions. Her mother's investments became an additional object of her prowess. In two short years, my mother-in-law's bank account was funneled into various endeavors. Through cleverly orchestrated maneuvers, it was made to look as though Emily and I had stolen the money. It had strained and all but destroyed Emily's relationship with her mother, her son, and her brothers. My heart breaks as Emily's tears fall, and between the sobs, she prays for a way to heal these wounds, a way to help her family believe we would never have hurt them.

Emily's mother was an only child, born to an eighteen-year-old, feisty Irish girl and a handsome, older Italian boy. Her first two years were happy, but her father increasingly enjoyed activities outside the home. The arguments and abuse escalating, she was sent to live with her grandparents, an arrangement made to accommodate her mother's work schedule. The emotional abuse leveled against her by her father and the abandonment she felt from her mother created a personality steadfastly entrenched in vigilance and responsibility. At age three, when you are learning your individuality and autonomy, you also need the safety to try these new freedoms on for size. For two years, she found her own way amidst a family that spoke no English in the home. She was incorporated into a household containing several aunts and uncles, an alcoholic grandfather, and no safety. The chaos was no less in that household than the one from which she had been removed. She was brought back home when her parents reconciled, but the abuse continued. Avoiding her father became her life's work; avoiding intimacy became the consequence. Emily's father, who adored her mother, when proposing said he could wait to be told he was loved because he could say it enough for both of them. And he did—to her mother and all his children.

When Emily's father died, her mother's anxiety increased, the safety she finally experienced with her husband was gone, and she retreated into the life of hypervigilance and social isolation once again. Her mother's identity stolen only proved what she had always known: the world was unsafe. It was, however, less frightening to believe that someone she knew would steal her money than to face the possibility her world could be invaded from the outside, leaving her without control. An impenetrable fortress was around the family, communication totally severed; this estrangement and isolation was yet another useful tool in the continuing ruse and illusion that had been created in our lives. The suffering inflicted now extended to the entirety of Emily's family. Emily and I mourned the loss of the love and support that we once trusted and cherished.

The oldest of five, my wife personifies the description of the first child in order of birth. Educated in parochial schools, she is responsible and an achiever. Order and discipline, particularly around home and money issues, provided safety and the freedom to enjoy the rest of her life. Bills are paid immediately; the kitchen and work areas have only one place for any utensil. Documents for any transaction—taxes, insurance, correspondence, and purchases—contained dates, times, contact persons, and any associated telephone numbers no matter how remote. The chaos injected through loss of financial assets and family support kept Emily agitated and in a panic as new problems surfaced daily with confirmations of loss and black marks on her credit rating. She viewed these difficulties as sins on her soul. Like Hester Prynne in Hawthorne's *The Scarlet Letter*, she thought the world could see the huge red BC on her chest signifying bad credit.

I needed tools to complete a project at the inn. Despite Wal-Mart's doors never having been darkened by her five-foot-two-inch frame, the check Emily wrote was rejected. It was explained that, five years before, a check was returned for insufficient funds. Of course, she had not written this check, and there was no doubt who was responsible. Emily was embarrassed and inconsolable. This mean-spirited body of hate was unstoppable, insidious, and destroying the peace in my Emily's mind.

The only solution Emily could imagine was her going to work. It would, in fact, solve most, if not all, of the problems. Her salary, until my inheritance was settled, would provide the necessary funds to secure a home, allowing me time to open a blacksmithing business. I couldn't tell her about the voice and the threats against her life. I needed her to remain where I could protect her, daily I had to convince her that the *best* decision was for her to continue to help me with the construction jobs at the inn. She never really understood, but in spite of her misgivings, she trusted me. She knew that my reasons would eventually reveal themselves. In the meantime, wherever we turned, whatever we planned, however we schemed, there were no roads of escape from our economic nightmare and the confinement of our little room at the inn.

Chapter 7

Vocation and Spiritual Commitment

I AM AN ORDAINED priest. I often say that blacksmiths need a hobby; my work at the forge gave me peace, a serenity that allowed me to glimpse the workings of the universe and the God who created it. It was a small step for me to dedicate my life. My night with my high school girlfriend was also instrumental in my decision. Returning from our date, running much later than my mother had approved, the words, "I've decided to become a priest" blurted from my mouth. These utterances, the ones she had longed to hear for sixteen years, removed any reprimand from Mother's lips.

Three years before my birth, a baby boy, my older brother, born to my parents had died suddenly. Desperately wanting another son, my mother promised to dedicate this second child to God if He permitted her to give birth again. "Even as Hannah dedicated her son, Samuel, to the temple and Eli, the High Priest, when the boy was six years of age" (1 Samuel 1:28). I was reminded from my earliest days of this bargain. With my declaration that morning, and a sigh of relief, Mom cried, "He has been chosen; praise God."

The priesthood was a natural progression of my metalwork. Working with my hands is fundamental to my life. It allows me to earn a living and give my time and talents back to the church. My personal concentration is on healing and the preservation of the ancient liturgy. My vows, my solemn promise to God, mediate my every decision. I have pledged tolerance of personal injustices while intolerant of prejudice or inequity toward others on my journey to become. As in the prayer attributed to Saint Francis of Assisi, Francis commands:

Lord, make me an instrument of Your peace.
Where there is hatred, let me sow love;
Where there is injury, pardon;
Where there is discord, union;
Where there is doubt; faith;
Where there is despair, hope;
Where there is darkness, light;
Where there is sadness, joy.
Grant that we may not so much seek to be consoled as to console;
To be understood as to understand;
To be loved as to love.
For it is in giving that we receive;
It is in pardoning that we are pardoned;
And it is in dying that we are born to eternal life.

My association with the civil rights movement took me to Selma, Alabama; in some small measure, I helped right an unconscionable wrong. My work with the ministry found me in Haiti, working to assist in establishing feeding programs and building a medical clinic. My willingness to share my time, energy, and money was evident to all who knew me. I took seriously the words of Saint James: "Show me your faith without deeds, and I will show you my faith by what I do" (James 2:18). "Anyone, then, who knows the good he ought to do and doesn't do it, sins" (James 4:17).

To the starving man, the words "I'll pray for you" make little difference; only a meal that nourishes his body can leave him open to a life that will nourish his soul. Maslow, in describing the journey toward man's self-actualization, recognizes in his hierarchy of needs that food, shelter, and clothing are fundamental to this process.

I have committed my actions as an illustration of my faith and love of God, endeavoring to provide human relief through whatever means available to me: time, money, emotional or psychological support, and spiritual guidance. God has blessed me with an inquisitive and intelligent mind, talents both artistic and mechanical, and a strong body. In the parable of the talents, Jesus said, "To whom much is given, much will be required" (Matthew 25:29). My commitment to God is my life's work; it is my vow.

Emily often tells me the story of my life:

> A Buddhist monk answers the monastery's front door to find
> a woman holding a child. Handing the child to the monk,
> she reports, "This child is your child." Without hesitation,
> he accepts this little one into his life, nurturing, loving, and
> educating him for ten years. Again, a decade later the same
> woman stands at the front door. This time, she pronounces,
> "This is not your child." He allows his son to go; it must be
> the will of God. His heart is aching, but he must obey.

"As the body without the soul is dead, so faith without works is also dead" (James 2:26). A modern rendering of this says, "Love without action is irrelevant." These mandates are the direct fulfillment of Jesus's teachings. In the only parable He used concerning the final judgment, the Eschaton, Jesus said, "You have done it to one of the lest of these, my brethren; you have done it for me; you are acceptable into the kingdom of God. But, if you have not helped these my brothers, you did not help me. Depart from Me ... into everlasting darkness."

Some years ago, my father received a request for a donation to a shelter for homeless boys and girls. Enclosed was a simple narrative supporting our responsibility to care for those homeless, hungry, and shivering children pointing out God made us to be his compassionate emissaries.

I have chosen to follow the commandments of Jesus and Saint James. A gulf as wide as that which separates heaven and hell existed between my ex-wife and me. Added to the ever-growing list of ways to haunt me was my theology.

In my verbal contract with the manager of the inn was my word of honor. I would help him improve the physical condition of his business to attract more customers. The increase in revenue would provide monies to pay me at a fair market price. I agreed to wait on payment. He agreed to pay me in a reasonable time. Like my mistake with my ex, I was honest and committed to my promise; it was not in my thinking that he would procrastinate his. I became essential to the development of the inn. The remittance of payment for my work became essential to my ability to leave. There was every incentive not to pay me.

Critical mass had been reached. Emily's spiraling anger and depression were gaining momentum, and my helplessness to console her in the midst of my trying to protect her constantly brought our attention to analysis and problem-solving. As a psychologist and my wife's experience as a family therapist, more specifically as a crisis clinician, the technical component of this exercise was relatively easy. Nevertheless, implementation of these solutions became another frustration, another nightmare. The more feasible our solutions became, the more creatively mean were the games. My ex-wife's genius took her maze of ideas to unimaginable places. Using every ounce of personal information about Emily and me, the latest in current events and—primarily—the inn manager's cooperation, she produced and directed an epic production rivaling even the 1939 blockbuster *Gone with the Wind*.

We were completely impotent before the onslaught of the Angel of Death. A middle-aged couple moved into the inn while they waited to close on their house. Ruggedly built with weathered skin portraying his identified profession, he was a contractor looking to start a new business. His wife, perfectly dressed with coordinated outfits in spite of living at the inn for several months, was an inveterate knitter with three children. We would soon become good friends. We visited them often in their room and later in their new home. Eventually he was transferred back from whence he had come. They pleaded with us to pack up our possessions and make the journey with them. They argued their house was large enough to accommodate us until we found a home of our own. A collaboration of all our artistic and creative talents would provide sufficient income to open a storefront.

The money owed to me was denied since he could not afford it. This, however, could have been dealt with at another time, even at some distance, but the threats against Emily's life heightened. The voice promised to enforce those threats should I tell Emily or make a move to leave. Implicit in the threat was an imposed silence that was not limited to Emily. No one else could ever know why we had to remain at the inn; they could never know how much we wanted to go with them. At every turn, it seemed the black forces that surrounded us made any changes in our situation impossible.

Watching the U-Haul turn right out of the parking lot made Emily's tears turn to sobs. Still, I couldn't tell her how much danger she was in. I knew we were more alone than ever. The only hope for escape had disappeared down Main Street. Our close relationship with our friends posed a monumental threat to the success of the Angel of Death's acquisition. If, physically we were out of reach with friends to insulate and protect us, her ability to gain information by tapping our phone and accessing our mail would have been compromised. At the very least, she would need some start-up time, losing valuable resources already in place. She had won this move. The stakes were high, the money was huge, and the game continued.

In spite of our failures in finding an avenue on which we could extricate ourselves from our dilemmas, we trusted Grandma's gift was ours; inevitably, it would be in our possession and we would be free. Telephone conversations with our "banker" and our lawyer supported our belief. We were constantly assured by telephone and personal visits by the FBI that our safety was cared for and they too were working to thwart the ever-present evil. It would not be for another year that we would discover that the telephone voices were the evil creations of my ex-wife's twisted mind. With her computer, she hacked into our telephone line. No matter what number I had dialed, the call would be forwarded to her number—and she would pretend to be whomever was necessary to get the job done. There, at her central command post, were all the impersonators who were, in reality the banker, the lawyer, and the FBI spokesperson with myriad other incidental and necessary voices.

Chapter 8

Parade of Characters

DURING THE YEARS of our discontent, an interesting array of characters passed through the office doors, and much of our free time was shared with them. A middle-aged man, our next-door neighbor, an ex-marketing executive, was there a year. We looked forward to our morning conversations over tea, discussing all the usual topics from politics to religion. He was a student of the colorful local residents; his telling of his nightly adventures at the OTB (off-track betting) establishment kept us in stitches. Our mutual dislike and annoyances of the manager were expounded upon at each greeting during the day.

Two doors down, a kind and sensitive woman shared in the roasting. Every day, a package would arrive from the Home Shopping Network, a moment in which she delighted and would anxiously await. Each week, when the rent was due, an argument over almost anything was bound to brew. Emily became friends with her, sharing the sadness of her mother's recent death, the decision to care for her ill father at home, and the struggle over custody of her three children. Her generosity of spirit provided an abundance of emotional support for Emily.

A young couple and their school-aged son and daughter stayed with us for many months. Their financial struggle was not unlike our own. Most of the husband's salary was consumed by the rent he paid at the inn and feeding his family. His work was an hour away, and fuel for his car was expensive. Saving the requisite amount for first, last, and security deposit to secure an apartment was impossible. Impossible, too, was the manager's willingness to give this family a lowered rent so they would have a chance to get on with their lives. After much cajoling, I was allowed to make a desk and a jungle gym in exchange for two weeks of their rent, the equivalent of roughly $700. It wasn't all they needed, but it was a start.

A car accident brought another desperate couple to the inn. His left arm was in a cast, and he was waiting for his first disability check, which was already six weeks late. His wife worked at the local department store— her salary all but gone after the rent was paid. They had arrived in the winter, but now that it was spring, the rent was going up. Unable to afford the increase and the usual unwillingness to let any customer stay for less, in spite of their faithfulness, they too were forced to leave. We were very surprised one rainy Friday night when they returned to tell us they had found a place they could afford and to thank us for the support they so appreciated over the months they stayed with us. We were not sure exactly what we had done, but we knew we cared about them and would provide a daily sounding board for their concerns and triumphs.

We looked forward to a fearless couple from Florida each summer. They brought with them stories of adventures that no sane individual in their seventh decade should be experiencing. They delighted in examining our art and hearing stories of our past adventures. Their daughter was depressed from the aftermath of a difficult divorce, but our clinical input provided them with ways to emotionally support her; relating Emily's own divorce experience gave them hope.

Arriving from a coastal community with their fur-ball dog, this couple showed up every March and October in cowboy boots and ten-gallon hats. They rented the same room, needed the same special chair for Mother for prayer and meditation, and wanted conversation in place of room service. His heart was giving him trouble, and he needed surgery, but we could only pray for him when the next March rolled around without their arrival.

For eight months, we were blessed with a group belonging to a crew working on a local project site. We loved having them there. They were sent off in the mornings with a wave, and at day's end, we looked forward to their return. Their personalities and histories provided many topics for conversation. They, like anyone who stayed at the inn longer than one night, had much to say about their follies with our manager. During one weekend away, one of the rooms had been rented without permission. The belongings and the contents of his refrigerator were put in storage; this customer's return on Sunday night brought one of the most unpleasant scenes and threats of a lawsuit. It was a potentially fruitless argument, and the rental contract was angrily ended.

Our friends had planned to stay until Christmas. These plans were squelched when it was announced the building in which they were staying would be closing in mid-November. No one knew the reason $2,000 a week in rent would be turned down. Their bill would increase the inn's revenue by $10,000 simply by leaving those rooms available for five additional weeks. It is now our suspicion that our friendship with them, like all the others, posed a threat. With sad hearts, we waved goodbye on the day before Thanksgiving.

He was quiet and a loner. He left for work early and returned after we went to bed. During a snowstorm, he and Emily talked. Divorced as a result of his years in the military, no permanent roots or established home separated them. He had no car and was always out of coffee, a desperate combination. An automatic coffee maker from one of the kitchens and an extra can of coffee that we picked up at the market each week solved his dilemma. Emily decorated his room for the holidays: Christmas ornaments hanging from a green hanger with homemade presents underneath, Valentine hearts, and Halloween candy brought a little feeling of connection and home. All his treasures tagged along with him when he departed inconspicuously.

All the rooms were in desperate need of refinishing. Out of work and as desperate as the rooms' need for paint, this young man had fallen into the clutches of the inn's manager. A bargain was in the making. The two agreed on a price, a contract was signed, and work was begun. Methodically and flawlessly, he applied the color. It was necessary for him to complete at least two rooms per day in order to be paid in time to meet his financial obligations, but the preparation time (removing fixtures, moving furniture, and reassembling the room) made this feat impossible. Emily and I, in our spare time, helped like little elves. Breakfast was brought to him unannounced, and a bathroom with clean towels was opened each morning for a much-needed and appreciated shower. He inherited the left-behind coffee maker. Our kindness was infuriating. Emily was berated only to be summarily ignored. This man was relegated to sleeping in his truck and did so until his first paycheck; he then paid his rent at a minimally reduced rate. In six weeks, he too was gone, leaving behind twenty beautifully painted rooms in a hideous shade of green.

The snow brought the snowplow man each winter. With each storm, regardless of the amount on the ground, the manager would call to say, "Bring your plow."

"Do you think I'd bring a screwdriver?" he'd reply. He confessed to keeping the inn on his list only because I was there to help. Should I ever leave, he vowed to never set foot on the premises again. More time was spent cleaning the inn's parking lot than any of the twenty other contracts he had. The manager bedeviled him, following beside the truck and pointing out areas that were missed. Should he leave without checking in, he would get another phone call to come back; it was never, ever good enough. The snow brought more work for me, but knowing I would see my friend the snowplow man made me smile. We could share the most recent and many past indignities dished out in both of our directions. He was saved only by his ability to go home.

The man who drove the Porsche occupied the same room for three years. He smoked cigarettes, watched television, and read the newspaper during the day. He was gone sometimes early in the morning and most evenings. We exchanged little more than a hello, but three days a week, an apology was extended. It was expected he vacate his room while it was being cleaned. This usually meant waking him in the mornings and invading his privacy to tidy up an already organized space. At our departure, he remained in the same room, his quiet ways still a mystery.

Local construction brought the renting of five double rooms. Ten Latino men of various sizes and with various understandings of English stayed for six months. They would have been there longer, but the manager was distrustful of foreigners and made their lives more than miserable. He would turn down their heat on cold days and turn off the air conditioners on hot ones. Telephones were shut off, and he denied them the use of the television remotes. He set aside special towels for their use. These towels were clean but stained and frayed. (This idea, which he perceived as brilliant, was implemented from then on for any customer who smoked or worked construction.) His frustration with the language barrier made him even more obnoxious. My limited command of Spanish helped ease some of the tensions these young men felt so far away from home. It was not enough, however. One Saturday morning, an argument over their rent brought their business to an end. A procession of the ten packed themselves into the van and headed down the road to the nearest motel. Handing us a large tip and an apology, they said, "Adios."

Fighting was the norm of the day. This couple were full of vinegar— or should I say beer. He didn't work, and she did, which was not a small issue between them. Fights over the alcohol and who paid, their paranoia that the other was cheating, and arguments over opinions on a variety of subjects usually increased the drinking and the abuse. The verbal harangues escalated to physical beatings. For two years, she tolerated the bruises, broken teeth, and facial cuts. She had him arrested, but like most battered women, she questioned her responsibility and participation. She and Emily spent many hours talking. The drinking didn't stop, her thinking stayed clouded, and finally she departed.

Each February, this couple met at a central location since they could never agree on whose home to make their own; their decision was complicated by the proximity of their respective families. Since he traveled for his work, these rendezvous were the perfect solution. She suffered from a variety of health problems, including insulin-dependent diabetes. Daily, the disregard for her diet brought a variety of problems: severe insulin reactions, circulation difficulties, and a near coma. Her room was always a stop on our morning rounds. Two weeks after their three-month stay, her daughter called concerned that her mother hadn't arrived home; she couldn't find her. We never knew if she was okay.

She walked slowly and hunched. Her sorrowful eighty-three-year-old eyes were tired; her husband of fifty years was hospitalized after a stroke. "He is my life," she said. "We never had children, and we spent all of our time together; maybe that wasn't such a good idea." Her husband, however, was expected to recover. The long days at the hospital tired her, but soon they would sleep in their own bed in the farmhouse they had shared their whole married life. Emily grasped her hands, and her eyes filled with tears when the words were whispered on Christmas morning: "I lost him." Emily held on to her shaking hands. Early the next morning, dressed in black, she left to say goodbye to her beloved.

Doors opened and shut as thousands of stories passed through. In some way, our lives were changed by each history. Some touched our hearts, some made us angry, some brought a smile, and some stirred us to act on their behalf. As significant as the thousands of customers, the men and women added value to the inn with their professional skills.

For the third time, the parking lot needed to be resurfaced. The crew of five that showed up on September 11, 2001, came early. Of course, they were admonished. "Nice inns don't make noise before nine!" he screeched.

The relationship with this group started out like all the others. As adversaries already, there was little room for any give. He stood with his arms folded in front of his chest, his face like a storm cloud, and his posture erect like a prison guard. With the intensity of my grandfather inspecting my work at the forge, he inspected each inch of the newly paved lot. His agitation took a new turn when I welded a part on one of their broken machines. By contrast, my friendliness made his unyielding dissension more obvious. The horror and tragedy of the World Trade Center collapse that day made no difference in the context of his needs. He tortured these men because they were taking time out to discuss and watch the television coverage, and probably more importantly, his visage was that of a Middle Eastern male. (This fear created the obsession to fly the largest American flag he could find, another problem that became mine to solve.) These five men paid no attention to his demands. They knew their business and did a magnificent job. At the end of the day, there was unused blacktop. In his usual demanding voice, he ordered, "That blacktop is mine. I want you to put it on the front parking lot."

It was a valiant effort, and they replied, "Are you going to pay us?"

"No."

They said, "No." The day was over at last.

At eleven o'clock that night, they were finally finished. The perseverance of the team of four carpet installers started the first of the contracted nine rooms at seven o'clock in the morning. At six o'clock, with the van packed, they headed to the office for payment. In keeping with his usual obstreperousness, he refused to pay. The health department had demanded the floor of the laundry room be carpeted; the current vinyl flooring was dirty and cracked. Linens would need to be rewashed if they fell to the floor. He, an opportunist, had the power, and the installers wanted their money. He demanded they lay the twenty yards of carpeting needed to cover the floor in the huge room before they were paid. It was their move. The power was now theirs, and they refused to pick up the flooring at the wholesalers. The stalemate was broken when I agreed to run the errand. Angry and exhausted, the four men relented. They were finally paid, and they were never to be heard from again.

"No job too small," said the ad. Remarkably, for all the other jobs he had completed, he had been paid most likely because the bills were so low—until the hot water tank fiasco. Leaving him alone with his work, the manager was confident that I would oversee the installation of the tanks. All went well, but not surprisingly, his payment was dependent upon removing the old tanks. There was no room in his van. He wasn't paid, and the tanks stayed.

The names and contracted services changed, but the scenarios played out monthly—if not weekly. There was not a plumber or an electrician in the surrounding area who would do any work at the inn; the professionals in the adjacent states and towns within close proximity had also been infected. The diminishing pool of tradesman was of minimal concern since I did many of the plumbing and electrical repairs and installations. His incentive not to pay me was further reinforced.

Like many of the other tradespeople, we were not being paid as promised. Frequently, we were asked why we stayed. No one would believe us if I reported that Emily's life was constantly threatened if we were to leave, so we simply said we were saving our money to purchase a home. The isolation, eventuated by the lack of freedom to speak of the threats, kept us in our prison. It appeared, however, that a release date was at hand. There were daily reassuring voices on the telephone from the banker, lawyer, government officials, and FBI confirming our plight would soon be over—and my grandmother's inheritance would again, and at last, be given back to me.

We knew only one thing to be true: Grandma loved me, provided substantially for me, and those monies were in my hands until they were handed over to the accountant. There was now, at this time, nothing real in our lives. We knew all about us was an illusion; we couldn't find the veil that covered the truth to pull it back. Confirmations reinforced the lies. We prayed, begging God for guidance, protection from harm, and a way out of this craziness. We kept to ourselves, thinking it was the safest way for us, for our family, and for our friends. We were afraid the identities of our other family members would be devastated like those of my in-laws. There was nowhere to turn. We could find no answers, and with each attempt at investigation, the threats became more frequent. The FBI reported the most outrageous information. Because the threats were supposedly independent of the protective arm of this operation, a balance could never be achieved. One problem solved was always counteracted by a problem in another sector. The threats would stop only when problems arose that precluded settlement of my inheritance. Conversely, the danger for Emily increased when it appeared there was a financial solution on the horizon.

Prior to our friends leaving, most of the problems revolved around the house that we believed would be ours someday. We were confidentially informed the owner had acquired her home with money from an inheritance. Reportedly, she owed taxes, and the IRS was scrutinizing this sale very carefully. Consistent with our Realtor's information, the house had been taken off the market. The lawyer reported that, in order to circumvent these governmental problems, she was pursuing a private sale to avoid the sales commission and increase her profits, ostensibly to have the funds to pay the tax. This house was perfect; we agreed to wait until her difficulties were resolved since my inheritance was still unsettled for us. These two themes—our shared financial problems and the threats to Emily's life—were the threads that wove their way through the perception of our reality, our illusion, tying all the other insanity together.

It was two and a half years more before we would finally leave the inn. Preparation for an infinite number of lies to keep us distracted and under control had to be made since the Angel of Death had no way of knowing how soon she could successfully gain control or my money and avoid getting caught. It was a perilous road she was walking.

Chapter 9

False Sense of Security

STANDING BEFORE A judge in court, I had been declared alive. It made no difference. My ex had notified every professional organization, university affiliation, artistic guild, and governmental agency with whom I had any association informing them of my death. But her genius rose to the occasion. Our lawyer informed us she was now arguing that, instead of being dead, I was simply missing. I was now MIA. As the wife, she had the right to contest my estate. Alleging the financial hardships she reportedly would endure by not receiving the inheritance was open for debate in probate court, but, as sole recipient of a recent substantial bequest, she was surely not without security. If you are going to sin, sin boldly. And she did. Her arrogant boldness was more than simple narcissism, but was/is the result of an arrested maturational development.

In adolescence, we find an inability to interpret any possibility of our mortality or negative responses to our actions. The teenager is self-absorbed. Arrested development eventuated by drugs or alcohol use, lack of appropriate discipline, absence of nurturing, or just consistent good luck allowed my ex-wife to continue to believe in her superiority. The crisis of adolescence, as argued by Erickson, demands coming to terms with your personhood and finding your place in the world. Without success, the destination is confusion. Her maturation seems to have been halted at some point before she reached the age of sixteen years. Chronologically in her sixth decade, her mental and moral developmental age is somewhere between sixteen and twenty. This sub-adulthood invincibility served to exacerbate her socio-pathology. Her arrested development stemmed from abuse suffered in the prepubescent years. The daughter of a psychotic mother and an emotionally absent father, she had been neglected, often beaten for those things her mother deemed as moral laxities. Knowing how to give and receive love evolves from the examples the child witnesses among the members of the family. Observing genuine affection between their mother and father is the most important gift a child can receive. This was not her experience. Her belief she would never get caught, her need to retaliate for all the wrongs she suffered, and the lack of structure she experienced by our separation was justification enough to continue to make me pay.

The voices this time, brought to us by the FBI, were a law professor and a representative from the Justice Department. These persons worked hard to convince us her claims were legitimate and legally sound. We knew this had no merit, but any telephone call we made was forwarded back to her, producing another confirmation of this idiocy. At one point, we insisted the lawyer make arrangements to give the inheritance to whomever was lusting after it. We anticipated this would bring the perpetrator forward, stop the chaos, and ultimately discontinue the threats. With this ploy, it became evident we were looking for answers in places that would expose her. The telephone threats increased; the FBI was poised and ready to assist as always.

The tragedy of 9/11 opened the way for the most creative of her ideas. Tying in the fears of the manager's Middle Eastern appearance and the need for increased security, the ruse was a mix of politics, espionage, and fantasy. Allegations surfaced that the inn was involved in trafficking narcotics. To make this appear real, crack cocaine was planted in one of the customer rooms to be found by Emily. The drugs—we were told by the FBI—were smuggled in by a group of businessmen who deposited the substances in the bed frames while occupying the rooms for the night. While minding the office during the family's many absences, I took cryptic messages and requests to pick up individuals arriving from Mexico, Colombia, and the Middle East. Visits from the DEA and the ATF (we even have their business cards) confirmed this illegal activity. The county sheriff's department sent two deputies during a family outing to inspect the patron register for a name that was known to them in connection with narcotics distribution. It was no big leap to believe that this recalcitrant individual was capable of these infractions, but they went too far when they asked me to spy. I refused; the threats became more frequent—and more graphic.

Concurrently, it was requested I use my expertise in linguistics to help the government. Through the special agent FBI spokesperson, dozens of opportunities presented themselves. Voices speaking a variety of familiar languages flowed through the telephone. This process was fairly innocuous, primarily needing assistance understanding the culture and religious implications of the American position in the Middle East. As a graduate student, I spent time traveling in Israel and the Middle East. The voices proposed a post as an emissary. This was purely academic; everyone knew I would never entertain that thought. This offer stemmed from assistance with a staged negotiation that the FBI had deemed a governmental success. For this to make sense, it is important to point out that I had worked for the government for many years in many different capacities. Such governmental requests were not unfamiliar to me.

During the Vietnam War, as a member of the clergy, I successfully negotiated a resolution with two Vietnam deserters who had sought church sanctuary. The soldiers surrendered without harm to themselves. As a psychologist and a priest, interpreting behavior and information for clarification is a daily occurrence. Depressed clients contemplating suicide expect my skills to be sharp to provide reasons for them to live. Parishioners in spiritual crises look to the priest to negotiate a way back to God. I helped the FBI when I could, trying desperately to understand but never knowing what was really going on. During those times of seeming cooperation, the threats slowed to a trickle; it was worth playing the game to have some peace.

We attempted to content ourselves with the situations confronting us since random confirmations from the outside came often enough. We would be told, for instance, in our early-morning conversations with the FBI spokesperson who felt these check-ins necessary to keep us informed about our safety and the progress toward the release of my grandmother's gift. She would uncannily be privy to the next managerial request for that day. Surely enough, usually before lunch, he would make the request they had predicted. It did seem that our surrounding situation had some veracity.

It came to pass that the inn's legal problems were beginning to surface. The manager confided he needed a lawyer, suggesting the difficulties revolved around money; he never mentioned drugs. These problems were, he reported, directly related to why he couldn't pay me. He admitted to playing with "funny money." My lawyer and the FBI called it "money laundering." My imagination easily conceptualized this possibility and his participation in these illegal actions; in fact, many of my business contacts suspected and expressed this exact opinion.

It was reported he needed financing for future projects and to pay the thousands of dollars he owed me. His illegal activities prevented him from finding legitimate means of funding; a parade of possibilities was investigated. Each unconventional avenue was exhausted. They ranged from wealthy family members to foreign banks and all the sordid choices in between. I was kept up to date about his consistent failures in procuring a loan—from him and the FBI. The tension between us was palpable. We fought daily, and his agitation went through the roof. The threats became more frequent and intense.

His brother supported the information fed to us. The phone rang on a Sunday night. When I answered, he said, "What was my brother up to? Was he doing anything funny?" He wouldn't expound on what "funny" meant.

I said no. To my way of thinking, his brother's behavior was always funny. I wasn't prepared to involve myself in that debate.

He asked me to call him if I noticed a change in his behavior. What was strange to me was his absence from the inn since he was, in fact, the owner. Previous holidays, birthdays, and weekends were occasions for him and his family to visit. For nearly a year, he had been obviously absent. It would be another six months before I would see him again.

When he finally showed up, his physical appearance was a shock. He had lost several pounds, making him look emaciated. His color was pale even with his dark complexion, and his eyes looked haunted. He unexpectedly admitted that he had just been released from jail. He said he was extremely angry with his brother for turning him in for money laundering, resulting in the loss of his financial interest in the inn. The terms of his release demanded he have no opportunity to funnel funds through an enterprise he owned. This allowed his brother, the manager, to legally obtain a controlling interest in his business. This explained his absence, at least on the surface.

He begged my assistance in helping him get information about the inn's illegal drug activity. He believed he'd been given up by his brother to cover up the narcotics stashed at the inn. He told us that the rooms in the back building were full of illegal drugs and that they were going to be distributed for the money he needed to finance the inn. Payback for his incarceration was at the forefront of his mind. This was more information and responsibility than I wanted, but it was exactly the same scenario described to me by the FBI, and Emily had found drugs in the back building. It was inconceivable to Emily and me that someone would admit to being imprisoned for or involved in criminal activity if it were not true.

The distrust between these two brothers, the paranoia of their personalities, particularly in the aftermath of 9/11, along with their inherent greed and duplicity, drove them to astonishing lengths, separately and together, to conceal their activities from each other. At the same time, they were compelling each other to confess some of their activities to me and jockeying to be the first to request my help. I refused to be involved in their intra familial rivalries or their inevitable confrontations with our legal system. The secrecy deepened between the two brothers. Without prior warning, he would show up at the inn, which he had never done before. All the antics of the two siblings and their families were commented on and confirmed by the voices on the telephone.

To our rage and surprise, money had been found—money reportedly from his illegal dealings—but it was not enough to pay me. It seemed he was able to pay off some of his bills and finance a new van, a second car for his wife, and a motor scooter for himself. For my consumption, I was told, even though some financial obligations could be met, he was three to four months behind on his bills. He appeared not at all worried when I pointed out to him that his vehicles could be repossessed. He indignantly stated, "They wouldn't do that to me."

In his novella *The Sign of Four*, Sir Arthur Conan Doyle has the famous detective Sherlock Holmes describe to his friend and colleague Dr. Watson the key to his method of deduction. Holmes said, "How often have I said, 'When you have eliminated the impossible, whatever remains, however improbable, must be the truth.'" Using Holmes's science of deduction, we examined our clues and eliminated extraneous evidence. From the telephone voices, the brother's actions, and our unexplainable confinement, Emily and I believed the Angel of Death was, in fact, their collaborator, inspiration, and—no less important—their banker.

I alone was aware my ex was responsible for the threats on Emily's life. I was also painfully aware that she possessed the capability and inclination to carry them out. However, we didn't know she was also the voices. Sorting out these entities and their respective contributions to the conspiracy would come later. What had she promised? What bit of blackmail had she over these people? How did she know they would succumb to their greed? How could she be sure I wouldn't be told? Did she recognize her own pathology in these difficult people?

She was more out of control than ever. She had enlisted these people into her evil scheme, making it further possible to control and manipulate our lives. The family made the best of this, and their trips increased, staging the preparation to take his illegal booty to other locations for distribution. Usually the night before, he packed his new van with boxes, covered them very carefully, and piled suitcases on top. We knew him always to slither around, but in light of his brother's revelations, this behavior had some context. The FBI begged that we allow him to travel and agree to watch the office to help them keep him under surveillance. They reported the whole family would be going to prevent suspicion and avoid the possibility of the car being searched.

This freedom for them notched more opportunities to torment me. The game, now more enticing, was also more dangerous. So many balls were in the air. Her precision and execution of this juggling act were impeccable, but keeping me silent and contained was becoming more difficult as we became more agitated and inquisitive. Remembering my protective response and commitment to my daughter, the next move was planned and executed skillfully and systematically. The manager's children were now incorporated in the ruse.

Chapter 10

Extreme Duplicity

THE FAMILY'S ABSENCE meant more work, but, more importantly, it meant peace.

This peace did not include peace from my ex-wife. To prevent our escape, the threats always escalated. The visits from various governmental personnel carrying the appropriate badges and identification also increased. The officers usually brought news of exploits at the inn, assuring us that the DEA's investigation would soon bring about his arrest. They attempted to further shock us with the declaration the manager's wife was party to this criminal behavior. With both mother and father possibly facing criminal charges like her husband, a new dilemma now faced them: What to do with the children? Our relationship with the two little ones was full of affection and concern. The FBI required our input, recognizing that we would not want the children to be subjected to any involvement with Child Protective Services.

Beautiful black eyes peered around the corner of the office desk; the eyes belonged to a diminutive two-year-old. She was curious about this six-foot-two-inch bearded man carrying a box of tools. I opened the carrier and invited her to investigate. It was the beginning of the love between us. Each day, braver still, she would find my tools and me. Handling each item and imitating their uses, she would ask what they were called in English. She knew no English, but I was able to understand enough of what she said to start communicating. Over time, a language of our own developed—a mixture of our two dialects and made-up words that only she, Emily, and I understood. Within the first year, Emily had taught her the alphabet and her numbers; she loved the stories we made up, and they sang silly songs together.

She, like the rest of the family members, had requests for things I should make for her. She would pat herself on the chest and demand,

"You make for me." Her favorite gift was a scooter I made from discarded parts and painted bright red and gold. The streamers flowing from the handlebars were magnificent. Until she was old enough to ride alone, a little voice at our window would beg, "Oottar, can I ride my scooter?" She couldn't pronounce the word *Sudra*, in her language, which means a person who can do everything. Her family would use the word when describing me. Either Emily or I would oblige—it was impossible to say no to her, if not because we loved her, then because of her persistence.

This little one was not immune to her father's meanness. A tool set was assembled: a hammer, screwdriver, and pliers. My little helper smiled as she accepted this gift and inspected each piece. It soon was no longer hers; her father had taken the tools and locked them in the trunk of his car for his own personal use. Like her mother's jealousy of my love for my daughter, this child needed to be punished for our affectionate relationship. His anger at my affection for her gave him another excuse to level emotional injustices against this little girl. In both of these psychiatrically impaired parents, their inability to differentiate themselves from me put their helpless daughter at risk for abuse.

All physical abuse is preceded by emotional injury and is occasioned by a need to assuage anxiety concerning the abuser's feelings of inadequacy. Fear of being a good parent in a normally developed psyche calls for a greater understanding of the methods and practices of good parenting. In those individuals with neurotically and psychotically damaged psyches, the mind externalizes the anger at those persons believed to be at fault for their deficiencies. In this case, the rage is directed toward the child whose very existence proves the distorted belief of inadequacy—hence, anxiety; hence, anger; hence, abuse. The very act of abuse occasions a new round of anxiety and anger since the abusing parent *knows* from external sources that such behavior is socially unacceptable. That unacceptable behavior forces the psychotic person, not capable of accepting responsibility for his or her actions, to displace that behavior by abusing the child again. Without intervention, this action pattern escalates, the abuse moving from the emotional to the physical and, quite possibly, to the death of that object of abuse.

We only suspected physical abuse until one summer afternoon. While walking back to the house with Emily after finger painting, she stopped. Pretending to hit her own face, she said, "My daddy hits me like this."

Trying to contain her horror, Emily quietly said, "No one is allowed to hit you. You are very special."

Enraged that Emily had been trusted enough to confide this mistreatment, the anger was projected and displaced onto my wife so his daughter was spared from his abuse this time. By prohibiting his daughter from contact with Emily, he could kill two birds with one stone. The all-encompassing punishment was perfect.

My wife was a huge problem for him. Emily's presence was the obstacle that prevented the incorporation of our psyches. His daughter's confidence that Emily would understand made her even more threatening. Conscious or not, his relationship and pact with evil was solidified based on the hatred of a common enemy.

As a female, she was not the favored child—even when she was the only child. The prince, a boy, was born just after his sister's fourth birthday. From birth, this male heir was dripping with gold jewelry and placed on display like a trophy. He was for all intents and purposes just that. This male child was the evidence of his manhood and his religious and cultural acceptability. Before, with only a female heir, in the eyes of his family and friends, he was an outcast. Within their family, without a male heir, he was regarded as shunned by the deities they worshiped. It must have been a huge sigh of relief for the fortunate birth of a son.

The prince took center stage, constantly being carried in the arms of his father or those of his grandfather. The women were rarely seen carrying the little boy. They could wheel him in his carriage, but the familiar touch of an adult's arms was primarily the male's prerogative. His sister was left in the background, along with her mother and grandmother, to do only those things that pampered the males, whether they were newly born or adult. She endured, with many tears, the encroachments by her brother into her private space and her personal possessions. Like her father and the tool kit we had made for her, nothing seemed to belong to her any more—not even her Oottar. In contrast, his son was permitted to stay in the office, the garage, and the laundry room to play games with me.

No one knows how he came to call me Yi or what that sound meant to this one-year-old. Whenever I appeared, he would raise his right hand, walk quickly toward me, and shout, "Yi, Yi." When he got within arm's reach, he would stretch out both arms to be picked up. Usually, his father would quickly grab his arm to lead him away. None of these familiarities were permitted to his sister; most often, she would smile shyly at me from behind the nearest adult, fearing some sort of reprisal should she approach me. Her new behavior, her reticence toward me in the company of family, was the direct result of the birth of her brother. Secretly, when no one was watching, she would stand close to me, slip her tiny hand in mine, look up, and say, "I love you, Oottar." I could be her Oottar only in these few special moments and in the quiet of her own mind. These two little ones will always hold a special place in our hearts.

Distrust and distain for the parents did not preclude our concern and affection for the children and their grandparents. We never knew his mother's and father's names. We simply called them Grandma and Grandpa. You could hardly see Grandma, literally and figuratively. She stood barely five feet tall and weighed no more than eighty-five pounds. Suffering from a major depression, she blended into the environment. She presented with symptoms of anhedonia (loss of interest in previously pleasurable activities), loss of appetite complicated by constant upset stomach, insomnia, and extremely poor self-esteem, which was not at all helped by her station within the household. It appeared that it was more than enough to do the cooking for a family of six, three times a day, but the care of the two children also fell to her. There was always an argument and conflict over what and when to eat, when to bathe, and when to go to bed. Each morning, until these issues were settled, the wails of a crying little girl rang out. After the addition of a grandson, this frail, tired woman of sixty-five negotiated with two.

We were always thankful for the delicious authentic Indian food that found its way to our table. Grandma, in spite of her busy day, would think of us. It was never apparent what motivated her to do this. Occasionally, it would look like a peace offering after one of my more horrendous fights with her son. Primarily, however, it seemed genuinely from her heart. She always touched her heart and smiled when she saw Emily and me. My increasing comprehension of her language was particularly important to her; like the children, she could now make her personal requests directly to me. Not needing an interpreter, she was assured of receiving the exact item she detailed. Her requests were simple at first: repairs of her favorite cooking utensils, fashioning a specially configured rolling pin to make her native pastries, fencing in her garden to keep the groundhogs away (she called them puppies), and then, her greatest joy, a gold-painted two-story prayer shrine.

I researched nuances of this sacred construction, producing a triangularly cruciform-hipped roof topped by a Mukhbar, the sacred finial that denotes a prayer shrine. There was obvious delight in the shrine, and Grandma prayed at it daily. Again betraying his jealousy of Grandma, he made only one facetious comment: "You need to put doors on the shrine so the gods won't escape." However, Grandma would not part with the shrine long enough for the doors to be installed. I suspect the gods escaped each night and returned obediently each morning.

In spite of his maleness, Grandpa was treated disrespectfully by his son. His chores included the laundry for the family and the inn. He took his responsibility seriously, folding the sheets and towels with the utmost precision, only to be chastised and called crazy should he miss a hair or spot. Suffering from severe leg pain, not relieved by medication, walking any distance or up and down steps caused him distress. The added burden of hanging clothes to dry in the basement made no sense; he was not allowed to use the industrial dryers for the personal wash.

Consistent with his son's insensitivity, Grandpa was also expected to cut the grass in the areas not accessible to his riding mower. He was given an old, ineffective sickle to complete this task. He brought his request to me. This day, he wanted a tool fashioned that would cut and chop difficult roots and shrubs. Of course, he knew I could and would make this for him. It took me two days to complete a two-sided implement, an ax and pick, the handle just the right size and length for his five-feet-six-inch frame. His strength needed to swing the pickax, I made it as lightweight as possible. He used it with delight until he came to me and confessed his son had given it away. He asked, and I made him another.

His relationship with the grandchildren was different from that of their grandmother; he was not expected to care for their personal needs, and he could be the loving grandfather. He took them for walks around the yard, swung with them on the swing that I made for him, and taught them about the simple things in life like grass and bugs and airplanes. It was clear that these adventures were the best parts of his day.

The exhilaration of the manager in jail made our heads dizzy; if this were true, the children and their grandparents were certainly a concern.

Their inability to speak English, coupled with failing health, made Grandma and Grandpa in need of protection like the children. Their son made inquiries regarding Social Security benefits and private and state-sponsored insurances. He confided that his parents were ill and might soon need these services.

This came as a surprise; it had been made clear to me the arrangement he made with his brother for his managerial position at the inn included the responsibility for care of their parents. Additionally, his parents seemed integral to the family's emotional structure and actual living experience.

The next weekend, our last weekend at the inn, the males of the family arrived spouting rage at their brother. They were anxious to tell me he was worried their brother might try to have his parents declared incompetent and placed in a nursing home. Concerned about potential legal problems, I was told they supported his incarceration. Further, Grandma and Grandpa would be safe with him. The entire family described concern, each offering to accept Grandma and Grandpa and the children into their homes.

In the early afternoon, a compelling performance, staged for my benefit, assembled the brothers and their father. They were unaware that, over the last years, I had learned their language well enough to understand all of what they were saying and the nuances of their interaction. They invited me to assist as they, in their native tongue, berated their brother for his lack of respect for their parents. They admonished him for putting the family and the business at risk by involving himself with drugs and money laundering, pointing out that to mitigate the damages for everyone, he should turn himself into the authorities. They feigned interest that the sentence imposed would be minimal if he cooperated. He was not unexpectedly furious, but he agreed to consider his options.

There were no drugs, no money laundering (at least none that the authorities were aware of or admitted to), no one had been in jail, there was no investigation, and the children and their grandparents were in no danger. The entire family had been snared by my ex-wife! What could she have promised that would have made them sell their souls to this devil? What price was enough to betray Emily and me given the kindnesses, patience, and craftsmanship we shared with them? All this and more became patently clear the next day when I suffered a heart attack. The price—we would later discover—was $50,000 each.

Chapter 11

The New Motel

EIGHT MONTHS PRIOR to this weekend, striking out on his own, the manager of the inn purchased another motel in deplorable condition. This property of nineteen rooms, ten condominiums, and four cabins was on an infrequently traveled rural route. It was close to a recreational resort, but it was not close enough to attract the weekend athletes. Given his cry of financial distress, this investment couldn't have appeared more ridiculous. His youngest brother and his wife would be the managers. This was equally as ridiculous; their command of English was as limited as their experience in management. The family, nevertheless, moved in, furnishing the motel and their home with bed and bath linens, tables, chairs, mattresses, and drapes from the inn. We could only imagine the conflict that must have arisen over this. In the seven months the motel was operating, their business was so poor that they went for weeks without renting a single room. When they wanted to travel, they simply closed up shop.

The need for multiple repairs at the motel became another source of contention between us. They insisted that I spend three days a week there until the property reached the standard I had achieved at the inn. Clearly, three days a week for ten years would not be sufficient to complete this task. At best, I was willing to go for a few days to repair those things that would continue to cause deterioration. Not surprising—I was set up. A "representative" from a local bank paid me a visit insisting that a loan would be issued for the inn and the motel if I would agree to complete the list of maintenance projects. The "FBI" encouraged—begged—me to cooperate, reporting the motel had been purchased with suspected laundered money and the "bank" was supporting and benefiting from the illegal activity. My assistance would help with their investigation. We were also assured that, upon returning to the inn, I would be paid the money owed to us. Emily and I agreed a few days away might save our sanity and yielded to their request.

We arrived at the motel late on a Thursday morning. We had packed the truck the night before, but we were tired and hungry after our four-hour trip. Opening the door to the cabin revealed a dirty room with a queen-size bed, a tiny, ill-equipped kitchenette and a small but clean bathroom with a shower. Emily started to cry. The room was so cold, there was no phone, the television barely worked, and we were hungry.

Within an hour, we were visited by the same bank representative to ensure we understood all the repair requests. He reiterated the loans would be issued and we would be paid for all our work there and at the inn as soon as we returned. The money owed to me was significant—certainly enough to pay cash for a house and savings that would sustain us until my inheritance was released. Emily and I made plans to complete the work as soon as possible and were excited and looking forward to the absurdity of one component of our life ending. After a short rest, we regained our sense of humor and our strength and headed for the office.

Not really knowing this newly acquainted male member of the family, we only hoped he was not like either of his brothers. Our hopes shattered, this needy, demanding couple fired their wants at us. These demands were an endless stream of time-consuming tasks that were added to the list already supplied by the bank. By Monday morning, we were exhausted. Realizing how terrible the past five days had been, we were headed back to hell. However, given the promises from the bank, we anticipated our time in Hades would be short. We believed after all we had endured, the last few days could be easily tolerable.

The phone was ringing as we entered the room at the inn.

"Call your lawyer," he said.

Contact with the voices always brought bad news. This time was no exception. The bank had reneged on its promise for the loan; ergo, I would not be paid. I was so angry that my chest was hurting and tight. I hung up on the FBI.

I had no reserve, no more tolerance, and no more patience. My body was railing against the constant stress. Within two weeks, I would have a massive myocardial infarction.

Chapter 12

Cardiac Event

TWO YEARS BEFORE, after returning from dinner, I experienced the same heaviness in my chest. It lasted about ten minutes. The pain was unfamiliar, but I often had indigestion after eating something sweet. I suspected this was more of the same. The next day, the ask-a-nurse service at the local hospital suggested I call the cardiologist whose name and number she had just given me. The doctor returned my call, and after a short consultation, he gave me a list of dos and don'ts to prevent the reoccurrence of my acid reflux. The pain all but vanished with these techniques. I put it out of my mind. A year later, the pain returned, mostly after eating but occasionally when I was upset. It was always relieved with deep breaths and drinking hot water. This chest pain, like almost everything else, became an issue for the manager. He was angered when I had to stop and rest.

Complaints of no heat were phoned into the office one very cold January evening. I went to check the problem and determined that the oil tank was low. He needed to call for an oil delivery. To save money, he bought the least expensive oil in town. This unrefined oil left sludge in the bottom of the tank; the gauge showed a quarter tank. He was enraged. "An after-hour's delivery will cost twice as much," he bellowed. "I am in financial trouble!"

I walked with him to the basement and explained the concept of the cheap oil and sludge. The tension increased. When I told him that my chest was hurting, he stormed out and screamed, "I can't deal with this!" The pain immobilized me, but when the discomfort finally subsided, I was able to catch my breath and leave the cellar. I was exhausted, but I still didn't suspect the pain was associated with my heart.

Our FBI contact called soon after I got back to my room. She was worried about my health. She reported the office was bugged; during a routine surveillance, she had heard him relate the incident to his wife. She was quick to assure me Emily and I were safe even though the threats to her life were still viable. I was always reminded of the threats. My health could not be an excuse to escape the inn. In retrospect, the possibility of being incapacitated by an illness was of grave concern; it would render me uncontrollable. The very thing they had feared the most—my freedom— short of my death was about to materialize.

The cardiologist was just another voice on the phone, and his diagnosis was shot from the hip. I suffered a massive heart attack, with complicating factors that hospitalized me in the intensive care unit for three and a half months. The evil had been elevated to new heights. It is evident my attack could have been prevented if I had been speaking to a real cardiologist (his name was that of a prominent cardiologist in the area). This greed and subsequent need to control my life all but killed me. Without remorse, unflappable in her pursuit, the threats continued, albeit in a more desperate form.

On that fateful Tuesday afternoon, standing before me in the emergency room, a tall man in a lab coat said, "When you get out of here, you must return to the inn if you want your wife to be safe."

While I was waiting for the cardiac catheterization at the hospital, a second man in a lab coat uttered the same words.

The pain was excruciating, but my mind was clear. Replete with my haunting, I announced that I knew who had sent him.

The tall man, shocked at my perspicacity, turned on his heels and exited the room. This existential moment revealed the abject horror of my ex-wife's personality, which has given rise to our designation of her: the Angel of Death. Who could she have employed, cajoled, manipulated, or intrigued to perform such a dastardly, immoral, and unconscionable act? Who were these perverse creatures? I also knew in that instant that I would survive. God and I had met her worst, and she had failed.

To be prepared for any exigency, necessity dictated this Angel of Death know if I were going to die to strategize her next attack. Emily, preoccupied with my illness and sufficiently frightened by the threats, would have the freedom to execute the next move. The prize almost won; soon, she would be rewarded for her meticulous attention to detail, her brilliant and creative trickery, and her mean and unconscionable conduct. Like the Wicked

Witch in the *Wizard of Oz*, I could imagine her wringing her hands with delight, intoxicated with her perceived success.

If I should die, her portrayal of the grieving widow would give her claim to my estate. She could surely preempt Emily; only she knew exactly where to find my fortune. If I lived, which was not her preference, she still controlled the board. A fraudulent death certificate to the proper agency, while harassing Emily in perpetuity, outlined the plan. She was forced to choose the latter, but her work was not finished. The Angel of Death was desperate and agitated, recognizing her course of action would need to be altered at a moment's notice, based on the course of my recovery. Emily was in more danger than ever, and my survival meant more than just my life; I needed to stay alive to protect my Emily.

Returning to the inn was of paramount importance to the manager as well. This proved to be no coincidence; the final piece to the puzzle was exposed. He and my ex-wife were partners, coconspirators. The nasty little man with his pathological desperation arrogantly demanded of Emily, "Sudra must come back here to supervise. I won't ask him to do any work until he is stronger. You, Emily, need to work from nine until noon then you can go to see the doctor. When he comes back, you can work longer."

Emily stared at him with amazement; in this moment of clarity, she understood. He feared the monumental loss of my expertise, the easy discharge of his laziness, and—most of all—the association pregnant with financial possibilities. Emily said, "No."

He continued to bark his orders as she walked away.

The doctors told Emily I suffered the undisputed mother of all heart attacks. The coronary artery that supplies the left ventricle was occluded before it bifurcates and attaches to the back and the front of the ventricle. Statistically, I should have died; 99.9 percent of individuals suffering this form of myocardial infarction do not survive the attack. God and I had a talk; I believed Emily's safety depended on my being alive. I survived an additional twenty-four hours before a successful quadruple bypass. Two weeks postop, I developed an infection in my colon that eventuated a colon resection. I have a pacemaker and had to relearn to walk.

There is a formula for predicting the length of recovery: each week in bed requires a corresponding month for convalescence. I am told it will be a year before I will be totally well. God and I are in negotiations about that right now. All those who participated in my recovery admit it is nothing short of a miracle that I am alive today to tell this tale.

I never lost consciousness, but from the moment of the heart attack until three weeks before discharge, I could not speak; a respirator controlled my breathing. For six weeks, I was critical and unable to participate in anything outside of the momentary decisions concerning my care. Heavy doses of sedatives and narcotics blurred the world as I knew it.

Emily was alone. She was scared. No one could—or would—tell her I wasn't going to die or the length and extent of my recovery if I should live. Four days postoperatively, despite my critical status, I had stabilized enough for her to leave the hospital and start handling the rest of our life.

Her first task was to call the lawyer, inform him of my medical condition, and discuss the inheritance and the will—should I die. The phone rang fifteen times, and then the call was forwarded. This number was not that of a "lawyer." The banker's name was real—I had met with him—but Emily's call to the bank yielded information for which she was not prepared. "That president had not worked at the bank for some time," the secretary said. The man I met that autumn afternoon, three years ago, was a bank examiner, a friend of the Angel of Death who positioned himself at the president's desk, in his office, in his bank. Emily attempted each of the numbers we had called over the years, and the outcome was always the same: a disconnected number, a new listing for that number, or dead silence.

From the telephone book, she found and called the real FBI. The agent informed Emily that there was no special agent assigned in their office or any other office. He further disclosed the inn was not under investigation—and neither were the owners or the manager. Further examination revealed my grandmother's inheritance was still out of everyone's reach; my fortune resided in the same abandoned account all these years. The malignancy of her desperateness suddenly made sense. Alerted by Emily's investigation she had been exposed, but undeterred and focused, she continued on her tear. My fishbowl existence in ICU made access to me impossible. The bull's-eye was now on Emily.

Our truck was in good condition. He had regular checkups and oil changes; he was my pride and joy. Within a few weeks of my admission, the truck was making strange noises and soon was completely unsafe to drive. It had been sabotaged—not unlike the two vehicles we previously owned. Emily's Volvo and my pickup were vandalized a month apart in our garage. Both vehicles were towed to the garage that had serviced all my vehicles for many years. The repairs were procrastinated. Impatient for transportation and determined to hasten the process, we showed up at the station, but my truck and Emily's car had been released. The police were informed of our suspicions, but subsequent to the investigation, they reported a lack of evidence to prove who had committed these crimes. No one was willing to help us in the little town in which we had lived for many years.

It happened again. A truck, given to Emily by a family member of another patient in ICU, met the same fate. This truck had belonged to the deceased father-in-law of a young man whose father was hospitalized and critical after his second stroke in six months. When he heard the story of our truck's demise, he offered his truck to Emily. His generosity was beyond measure and exactly what Emily needed. She was so grateful to be driving a reliable vehicle, owned by a mechanic, but she worried each time she turned the key in the ignition.

Like our pickup, the truck was parked in the hospital parking lot for several days and nights at a time. From three o'clock in the afternoon until seven in the morning, there were only sporadic security checks. During the day, the lot was crowded; anyone could easily vandalize Emily's new truck undetected and with impunity. And it was; the same sounds and grindings were soon resounding from that truck. It had become unsafe to drive.

Fortunately, my discharge date was set for two weeks hence, and friends Emily had made at the hospital provided the rides she needed to take her the two miles between the house and the physical rehabilitation center. The messages did not go unnoticed. Emily looked over her shoulder at all times, especially in the ICU waiting rooms since the areas were open to anyone at any time. She obsessively locked her room and her car, and she carried all our important documents and our small savings with her.

Emily was more depressed than before my heart attack. She slept only three hours a night, and coupled with a poor appetite and heightened anxiety, she lost twenty pounds in the first two weeks. Emily's deterioration was becoming evident to the hospital staff. They were worried about her insomnia; they called it "underslept."

In keeping with the hospital's mission to treat the whole patient and the whole family, Emily was encouraged to confide her distress. Feeling vulnerable and afraid, she bared her soul to my primary care nurse and sobbed her way through her fears. Relating the story of the two men who came to the hospital to threaten me, the staff became even more alarmed; they believed Emily was delusional.

In a meeting with me and Emily and the hospital personnel immediate to my care, suggestions were made for medications and counseling to help reduce the symptoms of a reactive psychosis. The subject was dismissed when I confirmed that these men did, in fact, exist. It was unfortunate the projections of the nurses' fears clouded their minds to the possible veracity of what they were being told. Hospital security had been breached if harassment of a critically ill patient was missed. We held no one responsible.

Emily was isolated and afraid. I couldn't speak, and I couldn't protect her. She had no friends close by, no family to confide in, and communication with the staff was now limited to conversations concerning my care. The staff felt Emily would benefit from a new medication for sleep, and a prescription was written.

Two nights were all that she could tolerate this new drug. Sleep was not forthcoming, and her head was foggy the following day, possibly preventing her from noticing anything out of the ordinary. She reported to the staff the medication was very helpful, and they all commented on how much better she appeared. She contented herself that she was no longer a "project" and flushed the remaining pills in the toilet. She was withdrawn and unreachable. Reveling in her important accomplishment; the Angel of Death had inflicted the ultimate damage. With Emily sufficiently frightened and under control, it was now a cakewalk to the money, she thought.

Plan A and plan B had been worked out in Emily's mind: A if I lived and B if I died. Both proposals were viable, and the preparation for their implementation changed daily, especially for the first three weeks.

At eleven o'clock on a Saturday night, Emily was told my blood pressure had dropped so low that they had to reinsert a ventricular pump to keep me alive; there was little hope that I would survive longer than forty-eight hours.

The doctor called my eldest son, suggesting he gather the family to make the inevitable decision to turn off my respirator. Ceaselessly, Emily prayed at my bedside; she softly whispered, "If you need to go to your God, I will understand, but if you could oblige, I would prefer you stay with me." She reminded me that I didn't need to be sick to protect her. She believed my myocardial infarction was the only way to stop the madness in our lives; subconsciously, my body knew that illness was the only way to make this craziness cease. In the midst of her prayers, a calm peace descended. Emily knew I would recover.

The next morning, the doctors and nurses smiled as they reported I had had a good night. With Emily, my five sons, and my daughter around me, the journey toward discharge—long and uphill—took twelve more weeks. Weak and sixty-five pounds down, I left my bed and traveled across the country to recuperate in the loving presence of my eldest son and his family.

What do you say when a miracle has occurred?
Thank you, God
For Your loving touch upon me
And upon those hands and hearts
Endowed with skill and compassion to perform
Your miracle in my life.

PART 2

This is the day which the Lord hath made,
let us rejoice and be glad in it.
—Psalm 118:24

Chapter 13

Understanding Evil

MADNESS AND EVIL are easy; sanity and wholeness take exasperating work. It is abundantly clear that most people opt for the ways that require moderate work (the path of least resistance), allowing their lives to swirl in mediocrity. In a sermon some years ago, I said, "Most of us wander in the moral swamps where good and evil are our constant companions. Once in a while, a few choice souls pull themselves from the ethical quicksand to walk the high road of superiority." In addition, "Most of us worry ourselves into nameless graves, while here and there, a few forget themselves into immortality."

"Wide is the gate and broad is the road that leads to evil and destruction, many find it. But small is the gate and narrow the road that leads to life, only a few find it" (Matthew 7:13–14).

Many individuals, for most of their lives, find it easier to live a life of moral marginalism rather than using their talents to fashion a lifestyle of correctness and moral integrity. Their psyches stay filled with memories—constant, vivid, and strong—of the slightest evil perpetrated against them. Their anticipations and anxiety about the future are inevitable and palpable.

There is another way to live. That way of life is described by Saint Paul in the New Testament in two places (both in his letters to the Church at Philippi). "I have learned in whatever state or circumstance I am, there with to be content" (Philippians 4:12). "This one thing I do: forgetting what is behind and looking forward to what is to be, I now press toward the goal of the high calling in Christ Jesus" (Philippians 3:13).

Saint Paul has just expressed the foundations for Christian existentialism, which simply stated, pays little attention to what has happened (placing the past into historical perspective) and disregards the future as that which may be planned for but not immediately grasped.

Anything we plan for the future may be changed or negated by the events within a different *existens*.

The Sermon on the Mount adds another definition of Christian existentialism:

> Do not worry about your life, your clothing, food, and drink. Observe the birds of the air; your heavenly Father feeds them. Why worry about clothes? Look at the lilies of the field, they neither toil nor spin—yet Solomon, in all his glory, was never arrayed like one of these. (Matthew 6:25–34, paraphrased)

Jesus concentrated on the moment and the imperative exigencies of that *existens*. He says, "Therefore do not worry about tomorrow, tomorrow will worry about itself. Each day, every *existens*, has sufficient problems of its own."

Existentialism concentrates on the existent moment, the *existens* in Greek (not what was, nor what will be, but what *is*). Six words from the Greek describe the existentialists' philosophy of *being* and *becoming*:

- The *archaion*, that which is the absolute beginning; an instant in time unexperienced but not unknown, reported to us by the "Fathers," the "Old Ones" (in the southwestern Navajo culture, "the Anasazi").
- The *proteron*, that which is from the beginning (big bang, creation, that which we usually termed history), down to the immediate instant.
- The *existens*, that which *is* (the "beingness" of being, the essential and incidental now). It is necessary here to discriminate two important philosophical words: The *incidental*, that which is core essence, necessary and immutable (internal to the psyche; that which makes a thing, a person, what it is); the *accidental*, those qualities projected by the essential (incidental) and observable within the external world; for instance, in the Eucharist, the body and blood are the incidents; bread and wine are the accidents.
- The *eschaton*, that which will be from this instant, to the end of time (that which we understand in the future tense).

- The *telon*, the ultimate limit and/or end of all human *being*.
- The *ginomon*, the becoming; the process of successive instances that together make up the proteron and the eschaton and that single immediate instant that is the existens.

Forgive and forget are the existentialists' watchwords for the past. The ending, the finality of all that plagues (acts committed by him or against him) are completed and closed in the *existens*. These are not occurrences from outside the psyche; these are the existentialists consciously willing, in the existent moment, the finalization of those historic experiences.

This is "closure" (to use a popular, modern concept) in its finest expression. No closure happens from without (outside the psyche); closure is a willed act from within. Outside events, changes in relationships, and the mobility of situations do not affect that true finality (only the individual can).

Her daughter had been raped; her life and that of her daughters were irrevocably changed for twenty years. These two women, psychically joined in a common mission, pursued their elusive tormentor. Finally, after years of waiting, their "devil" stood at the bar of justice, condemned for another crime, for which he received a life sentence. Neither the severity of the sentence nor their ability to confront him were sufficient to "close" the events that occasioned their twenty-year odyssey. They still felt empty, and they were still victims because the only ending to their victimization and anger lay, as it always had, within their power to will.

The car, as she was backing from the garage thumped. Driving forward a little, she felt another bump. She stopped the car and got out to see what she had run into. Imagine her horror in seeing her son lying dead in the driveway, having been run over twice. Many years later, she could neither stop crying over the incident nor forgive herself for what had happened. She told me she was a good mother and could not be held responsible for his death. Her inability, in each succeeding *existens,* to accept the reality of the events surrounding her son's death made it impossible for her to heal.

The facts were simple: she was a good mother, and she made a mistake. A moment of inattention, a distraction, caused the accident, and it was an accident. At every moment during the preceding years, this woman held the tools for healing in her hands: stopping her mind's penchant for reconfiguring history. Denying any participation in her son's death because she was a good mother and admitting her culpability would have instantly healed her and brought closure.

We tend to compartmentalize pain into that which is psychological or emotional and that which is physical. It is an interesting phenomenon. We, as human beings, choose to revisit, understand, and reevaluate psychological pain while the distress caused by physical trauma is usually permitted to heal and disappear on its own.

Pharmaceutical research has developed an arsenal of medications to eliminate physical and psychological discomfort since both sets of symptoms may be debilitating and interfere with our ability to function effectively during the period of recovery. Additionally, alcohol, hallucinogenic drugs, and other illegal drugs are often sought to further deaden our traumatic experiences, but painkillers for both psychological and physical trauma contain inherent inappropriate and addictive side effects.

It must be remarked here that physical pain often contains an emotional component so the pain, like the revisited accident/incident continues unabated. At every moment, individuals have the ability to will their responses to either of these two pains and the closure of their histories and continuances. If one does not interfere with the history of psychological trauma, it—like the physical distress—subsides and disappears.

No one would suggest on the annual anniversary of a broken leg I should revisit the scene of my accident and break my leg again to experience and understand my historic pain. Since some individuals thrive on self-pity, psychological revisitation and reinvigoration of their emotions are common practices. It is antithetical to any healing process. The leg treated and healed; the pain will subside. Likewise, with treatment and therapy, the injury to the psyche will heal, and its pain will subside. The present is infected by the past—not because it is a natural course of events but because we want it to be.

Anxiety, depression, unhappiness, pessimism, and generalized angst are that which many people consider a *realistic* approach to life. It takes absolutely no energy to be pessimistic or depressed. We have been taught there are good psychological reasons for our negativity, and should we experience painful trauma, an infinite amount of time and effort will be required for psychic healing.

Joy, on the other hand, like optimism and happiness, is the path of adventure and bravery. Rather than choosing the ecumenical togetherness of pain, the comfort and pity of victimization, or the narcissistic pleasures of depression, the truly existent individual embarks on a journey of hope and optimism, a heroic choice every person can, and must, make. The existentialist mantra is as follows:

- Depression is cowardice; joy is adventure.
- Depression happens; joy is created.
- Depression invites solitude; self-pity invites attention.
- Joy allows the spirit to stand alone.
- Depression is narcissistic egotism; joy is wholly altruistic.

Depression, while demanding energy and attention from the self and all surrounding selves, contributes nothing to psychological or physical health. Rather, depression negatively adapts the individual, causing mental illness and physical devastation. Joy, on the other hand, asks nothing of anyone, not even the self since once willed it creates an energy of its own and contributes to the psychological serenity while promoting healing and health. Certainly, there are incidents in life, in varying degrees, that cause pain, suffering, and loss, but even here, there is choice—a choice as to our reactions to, and our interpretations of, those traumatic events.

Here, the existentialist discriminates that which is incidental to "being," and that which is accidental to the self. By interpretation, the self incorporates these accidentals within the psyche by internalizing pain, grief, and loss. However, these are foreign elements. While depressive and dangerous, they do not—and cannot—threaten our existence unless we allow them to become internal incidents. This discrimination between accidents and incidents is a choice within our control and is extremely vital. I can will, in every situation, not to see myself as a victim, but I will see myself as healed. Will I surrender? Will I feel sorry for myself? Will I act so other selves will feel sorry for me? Will I wallow in the mud of self-pity? Alternatively, you can handle the pain and see it as it is: an accident of life that will pass and within which joy is possible.

Physically, we know in every trauma, this side of death, the body immediately sets itself to correcting the situation: T cells, antibodies, adrenaline, dopamine, and endorphins rush to excite cells to healing, attack intruding organisms, cover gaping wounds, and put the body back on track. This is equally true psychologically and emotionally. Our psyches, after the needful time and steps for grief work, and without our continued intruding thoughts of self-pity, they are just as capable of healing as the physical organism. We have learned to meddle, exhaustively talking about our pains, our need to feel our trauma, and the necessity to experience the loss, all encouraging pity and solitude. With support groups and excessive time expected for recovery, we procrastinate our mental health. Our psychic illnesses are so satisfactory, and they feel so good.

For most people, closure is that which they expect will come from someone, or something else, from outside their personalities. However, since that never happens, self-pity deepens and the consequent anger only increases. This resultant depression stems from an inability or unwillingness to face the *isness* of the now. Rather, they wish desperately to reconfigure the past and manipulate the future, regardless of how impossible those historic and prophetic endeavors would be.

One need only mention a few examples regarding the extremes to which most individuals will go to find external closure: the relatives of the victims of the Oklahoma City bombing, the survivors and families of the tragedies of the World Trade Center, the fathers and mothers of the children killed in the several school shootings of the past few years. Most have cried on television, followed their protagonists' legal adventures, made vicarious careers of their relative's misfortunes and deaths because they were constantly seeking some external pronouncement of finality, a verification of closure. In the extreme, the family and friends of those murdered often demand death as the only acceptable justice—death, legally inflicted by the state, in the name of those victims. How can another's murder produce good feelings? How can the lengthy obsession with the arrest, trial, incarceration, and ultimate punishment of a defendant eventuate healing and peace? Since it is impossible to know, one wonders if the victim looks down upon us with thanks that we have given up our joy on their behalf. In all these cases, closure was entirely within their grasp, within their will. At every moment in the time interval between the affecting tragedy and the now (the *existens*) they could all have experienced the peace of true closure. Victims of trauma may not want to end their pain, but it is monumentally true that they can.

In Hebrew, *shalom* is an enigmatic word. Its most simple meaning is *peace*. In reality, its depth of meaning is almost fathomless. It indicates a series of events that begin the disruption or dissolution of a particular lifestyle. For example, in 586 BCE, when the Babylonians took the Jerusalem Israelites captive, few among the captives rose to power within the Babylonian Empire. After a period of time, those captives returned, rebuilt the Temple, planted their orchards and crops, and lived much as they had before the captivity. This latter end is denoted by the single word, shalom, designating restoration, peace, and tranquility. Shalom is an individual whose life has been destroyed by years of flagrant alcoholism, whose willpower survives detoxification, and sanity is restored. It is the life restored to wholeness after release from the Nazi concentration camps. It is the soul's joy and thankfulness experienced after the process of grieving the loss of a beloved. This is shalom; this is closure.

Chapter 14

The Psychology of Closure

E PISTEMOLOGICAL PSYCHOLOGY TEACHES us that, even in the present, nothing is experienced directly or immediately. Seeing may be believing, but what is seen may not be totally or externally true. It is an adage from my youth that one must not believe anything you hear and only half of what you see. Eyewitnesses, as we well know, are notably unreliable. All knowing (cognition) is the result of sensory data (from the outside) passing through our highly self-protective receptacles of touch, sight, hearing, smell, and feeling.

As an example, let us look at one of these sensory experiences: sight. Light transmitted through the lens in the iris projects an inverted image on the retina. This inverted image is translated at the retina into neural impulses (something like small electrical charges) along the optic nerve, moving through neural pathways (actual nerve fibers covered by the myelin sheath). These impulses jump across synapses (the unconnected ganglia) of neural fibers to a new pathway to be perceived at the perceptual centers of the brain. Here, the electrical/neural impulses are reconstructed according to categories of thought the mind possesses. The inverted image is reinverted since the brain believes that is the way it should be (that up is up and down is down, whatever that may mean). Anything along this line of transmission, affecting the myelin covering—illness, dietary insufficiencies, anxiety, or any of the diagnosable categories of psychosis, degenerative synapses that cause messages to be lost, scrambled, or detoured, and the limited number of cognitive categories the mind possesses—adversely affects cognition. This is true for perception/cognition in the present.

Memory, a revisitation of past cognition, is further complicated, leaving the individual with an additional distortion—beyond the initial distortion—of what he thinks he remembers. Each memory instant, each attempt to recover the past is to revisit the originally distorted perception, using the same self-protective and unreliable sensory apparatus devised and the cognitive categories that were initially used. Each memory, then, is an exponential revision of what was.

The past evils for which individuals seek recompense, revisited over the years, bear little resemblance to the actual occurrence. Harboring these malevolent historical distortions leads to almost insurmountable anger and evil. Checking the facts, however, usually leads to a highly different scenario than that which they remembered. Assistance in confronting faulty memories only increases agitation because the ego admits no such flaws. The subsequent approach to the future is then based upon their needed recompense: revenge. I offer an original poem to illustrate my point.

> What a deception; what an arrogance
> That my perception
> Of the "out-there world"
> Has any coincidence
> With the "really there."
> My controlled reception
> Of everything beyond this ellipsion
> Of my total self,
> Passed through myriad neuron pathways,
> Across synaptic abysses
> Reconstructed at the whim
> Of homeostatic/narcissistic self-indulgences
> I form worlds of supposed/proposed "reality."
> And so do you.
> With these projections,
> From within, bared souls, stripped even more bare
> Of external verification;
> So the miracle persists:
> That we communicate at all.

The psychological milieu of the early 1980s illustrates this memory distortion. The teaching community, child welfare agencies, counselors, and therapists all were concerned with child molestation and abuse.

Therapists attempted to recreate memories of childhood sexual abuse in their clients. Where these memories were difficult to reconstruct, counselors used hypnosis and suggestive therapy to help the clients remember. It was not long, however, before researchers and clinicians alike came to the realization that these recovered memories were nothing more than therapeutic suggestion and clinician projection. Indeed, one could argue the case that recovered memories on the part of any client told us more about the early childhood experiences of the therapist. The suggestive approach of misdirected social workers and family therapists only served to distort already scrambled memories.

One prominent child psychiatrist, defending a recovered memory approach explained that those who fail to admit sexual abuse as a child are denying the abuse or haven't yet realized it. Such a remark is ridiculous because of its absurdity and is, in all probability, a cry for help. She, with a significant following of therapists, and individuals craving an opportunity to assign blame to someone other than themselves, believed the lost memory of abuse was a result of massive denial. With a little cultivation, the nonexistent memory could be restored. These therapists engineered the revisiting of traumas that had never happened.

In one of my group therapy sessions, a female client succinctly remarked after ten years with the same therapist, "My counselor tells me the only explanation for my being depressed is that my father must have molested me." With her therapist's guidance, her search recovered only one incident when, as a five-year-old, she was bathed by her father. She believed, with this memory, she had found the source of her inadequacies. The accusations of molestation she then made, despite the lack of evidence, were justified in her mind. These memories were causing chaos in her family of origin and—more importantly—in her relationships with her husband and children. It took many confrontations with other group members to help this woman realize that her previous therapist had not served her well and her depression was a result of factors she was unwilling to face. The psychic damage done to these clients and their families is almost insurmountable. In addition, given the tenacity of the therapist's approach, clients recalling no such abuse became psychologically depressed when they could not remember, their guilt exacerbated because of their inability to please the therapist by not remembering.

The reconfiguration of history, which the existentialist knows to be impossible, also permits the client to deny responsibility, hoping to escape the consequences of his or her actions. To assist, the psyche rearranges the past as though it had never happened—instead of creating a nonexistent experience. Hence, for these clients, history has been rewritten.

The existentialist does not deny history or the past, realizing that he or she is the culmination of all those existent moments that preceded that fleeting *now* called the *existens*, each moment passing, like the separate frames within a motion-picture film onto the future instance. This is that continuum the existentialist calls *becoming*. Again, I offer an original poem.

Fleeting glimpses,
Forms perched in the air
Above my shoulder, dreamlike fantasies,
Awakened, when not asleep,
By some siren song
From long dead,
Eternally yet unborn, lips,
Jason before the mast,
Deaf, yet hearing,
Blind yet seeing,
Unexpected vistas little understood,
Time within time,
Consciousness within the unconscious,
Warped into a single reality—
Inseparably different,
Inextricably the same,
A continuum without tense,
Life arising, falling,
Phoenix, the plumed ash,
Charon, conductor and conducted,
Anubis, holder and the released.
Damnedly redeemed souls
Whose ankh-ka force
Distills dew-like,

Within the ether;
Ether-real phantasmic patterns,
Intruding thoughts,
Visiting where I have never
Again.

Chapter 15

The Existential Now

THE EXISTENTIAL CHRISTIAN is aware that something soteriological happened at an instant in the past, the culmination of that historic instant he believes will occur in some future existens we now call eschatology. But he does not ask what was real, what will be verifiable, or what the reality of those events is now. Theologically, historically, and scientifically, we wrestle with Jesus's death and resurrection. Our verification of this history comes in the words of those who witnessed those historic instances (New Testament).

Contemplation surrounding the veracity of those witnesses and those events, they report, are necessary academic exercises as attempts at extracting historical truth from separated existens events. These academic exercises also produce tremendous angst within the normal fellowship of the Christian Church. Again, the question for the existentialist Christian is not what was or what is to be—but what those events mean to me now.

The earliest disciples were, at the moment of Jesus's death, mired in their own histories and expectations of who Jesus should be and their own needs concerning Him. At the Crucifixion, except for John and a few women, all the disciples had fled in fear. In the days succeeding Jesus's resurrection, those same disciples reported physical confrontations with the Man whom they thought was dead. These appearances of Jesus, beyond uniting the disciples, seemed to have made no psychic or practical differences in their lives. Jesus's final commandment, to wait for some ethereal power, the disciples interpreted to mean staying together in the room in Jerusalem where they shared the Last Supper—praying and meditating on the life and ministry of their Lord and Master.

Finally, after fifty days of ceaseless meditation and prayers, an extraordinary event took place (Pentecost, CF, Acts 2). Suddenly, they felt as though a wind had swept through the room. Their hearts and souls became strangely warmed. This experience was described as cloven tongues of fire resting on the heads of each of them. The resurrection experience became real to them; it nerved and transformed them. Still, while little understanding either Jesus's death or resurrection, these frightened disciples' lives became instantaneously changed. Their personalities were transfigured into fearsome power and authority. It was this event, in the existens, that both validated what had been and prepared the way for all that was to be.

Within fourteen years, these disciples who had feared so greatly for their own lives had marched with the message of the Christ's resurrection to such an extent that there was not a part of the then known world that was a stranger to this Gospel. Those who had faced life with temerity, now, as a result of an existential confrontation with the resurrected Jesus, interpreted by the Pentecost event, transformed their lives. The miracle is not the resurrection (a historical event?), but the immediate confrontation of each disciple with his risen Master. All this—the transformation of the disciples and their swift evangelization of their known world—was the result of faith. It is a fulfillment of the words from Saint John: "To all who would faith Him, to those faithing in His name, He gave the right to become children of God; children born not of natural descent, nor of human decision, or a husband's will, but born of God. In this way, the Word becomes flesh and dwells within us" (John 1:12–13).

The mistake the subsequent Christian Church would make was making and trying to recapture that one event—Pentecost—rather than assessing that descendant power of the Holy Spirit in the immediate moment.

The same difficulties exist for dealing with the future. Prophets certainly have and do exist, but the extent and veracity of their purview is highly questionable. The many utterances of first, second, and third Isaiah—perhaps fourth and fifth—regarding the coming Messiah were interpreted quite differently among the three major related religions. For the Jews, the Messiah, in any of His aspects (warrior king–like David; suffering servant-like Jeremiah; teacher, insurrectionist, priest) is yet to come. For Islam, the Messiah may have been Mohammed, or like the Jews, He may be yet to come. For the Christians, the predictions are identified with Jesus of Nazareth whom the early believers called the Christ (Christos in Greek, Meshiach in Hebrew, Christ in English). This, each religion must do for itself. It is not a historic exercise or an unfulfilled future prediction; it is an immediate, contemporaneous identification in the now.

Future identification of events such as the writings of Nostradamus and the Apocalypse in the New Testament, because of their necessary vagueness, are open to wide varieties of understanding. Their prognostications, because we have no way of *being* in any other existens but this *now*, are pure fantasy at best, misleading deceit at worst.

The existentialist Christian does not fall prey to the monumental mistakes made by the early Christian Church in Jerusalem. These Christians placed their entire confidence in a futuristic interpretation of Jesus's words: "Some of you will not see death until I come again." Many of them sold their property, handed over their money to the church leaders, and lived in an expectant socialism, breathlessly awaiting the return of Jesus. But their predictions were ill conceived. Communicants died, money and resources ran low, and the small church at Jerusalem pleaded for assistance from the Gentile churches founded by Saint Paul.

There is an interesting Hebrew myth-story from the book of Exodus in the Bible, the Torah in Hebrew manuscripts. Subsequent to their escape under Moses from the land of Goshen in Egypt, the Israelites arrived at the Jordan River in Palestine. They had been ordered by God to cross the Jordan to enter Canaan. But the sons of Jacob, fearful because of their lack of military expertise, hesitated at the river and sent spies into the land to reconnoiter their prospective enemy's strengths. God, in the myth, angered at the lack of faith evidenced by the ten spies' reports the inhabitants of the land were too strong to invade, ordered Moses to tell the people that no one, except for Joshua and Caleb who were faithful to His order, would be permitted to enter the promised land: Canaan. They would wander the deserts near Mount Sinai until the last faithless Israelite had died.

God's demands emphasized an important existential requirement: seize the moment or forever wander in endless mediocrity. God provided for the nourishment of his Chosen People while they wandered the wasteland of the Negev. Every morning, a sweet white substance formed on the low branches of the few trees that surrounded the Israelites. Moses ordered the "people" to gather this sticky food called *manna*. The word comes from two Hebrew words: *Mn* "what" and *Ha* "this." The definition reflected the

Israelites' question when they first encountered the white sticky material: "What is this?" Manna tasted like coriander seed and could be formed into biscuits or flatbread or eaten as they found it at whatever place it was gathered. The Israelites were further ordered to collect only what they needed for their families for each day. Anyone trying to horde the manna found that it spoiled within a few hours. In addition, God provided flocks of quail to provide supplemental sustenance. Again, they were ordered to take only what their families needed each day since any surplus would be ravaged and useless. The lessons of the wilderness were lessons of faith: they are perfect examples of existentialism, what is now is important, and trying to preserve the now is fatal.

There is another Hebrew myth, regarded by most literary critics as one of the most magnificent compositions from the ancient world. This composition is simple: the first two chapters and the last chapter are a prose folktale outlining the devastation of Job's life and fortune at the hands of evil. In the last chapter, Job is rewarded for his faithfulness by resuming his place of honor among men and having his family and wealth restored. The scenes within the prose are artfully drawn. The devil confronts God with a proposition, saying, "Take away all that Job has and he will curse You."

God answered, "You can do whatever you wish, as long as you spare Job's life."

Job's esteemed place in society, his wealth—he owned seven thousand sheep, three thousand camels, five hundred yoke of oxen, and five hundred donkeys with many servants to care for them—and his seven sons and three daughters all were decimated by the devil in a single day. Our demons and the Angel of Death were less efficient; they needed ten years. Again, in the folktale, the devil appears before God. In the interview, God reminds the devil that, despite his calamitous misfortunes, Job did not sin or curse Him.

The devil offers one more proposition, saying, "Let me make him sick, close to death, and he will surely curse You."

God gave the devil leave to afflict Job—but not kill him. Job's entire body became plagued with boils. In his pain and misery, he sat on the ashes of his campfire, scraping his sores and listening to the ranting and ravings of his wife. His wife told him to curse God and die.

Job responded, "Shall we receive good only at the hand of God?"

It is simply stated in the Bible: "In all this, Job did not sin."

There then follows a long and extremely fine Hebrew metric poem that asks two questions: "Can a good God create an evil world? Why do the righteous suffer?"

Three of Job's *friends* (Elihu, Bildad, and Zophar) appear to question him. At first, they counseled Job that his present maladies must be the result of some secret sins he has committed. Job denies it. Again, they ask him to consider that his distresses may be the result of God's testing to make him strong. Although this would become a part of later Pauline Christian doctrine (a theological perspective I would deny out of hand), Job refutes the premise that evil is God's refining chastisement.

God speaks to Job and shows him the grandeur of His creation. While refusing to answer Job's questions regarding his miseries, God simply responds, "It is not right nor proper for the creature to instruct or question the creator."

Again, "In all this Job did not sin."

In Job 42, the prose folktale resumes. God blessed Job, restoring his good name, his family, and his fortune. "After all of his captivity, Job lived one hundred and forty years watching over four generations. Then Job died, being old and full of years."

This composition, with all its drama and questions, is a magnificent rendition of the existentialist philosophy and theology. Job did not bemoan or attempt to reconstruct his past—even when urged by his three friends and his wife. He made no attempt to lose himself in some future fantasies; he lived each existens to its fullest.

A favorite Yiddish story tells of a young student questioning an ancient rabbi. "With what perspective should I live my life?"

Hillel replied, "Live as though you might die tomorrow."

The inquisitive student haughtily asked, "How will I know which tomorrow will be my last?"

The rabbi responded, "Live every day as though it were your last."

This is existentialism.

There is another story from the Yiddish culture of Eastern Europe and Manhattan in the United States that illustrate the faith and optimism of those people known as Ashkenazi Jews. A famous rabbi, teaching on the streets of a small Polish village, was confronted by a conceited youth. The young man had captured a small bird and held it closely in his hand. He said to himself, "I will ask this wise old man if the bird in my hand is dead or alive. If he answers that the bird is dead, I will open my hand and let the bird fly away. If he says the bird is alive, I will close my hand, crush the bird, and then open my hand again to show him and his audience the dead bird."

Clearing his throat and holding his hand high in the air, this arrogant youth said, "You are so wise, old man; tell me is the bird in my hand dead or alive?" The old rabbi turned slowly, not to be confounded by the young man's trickery, and said quietly, "If I say the bird is alive, you will crush the life out of it. If, however, I say the bird is dead, you will open your hand and the bird will fly away. You hold the bird's fate in your hands. As you will, young man, as you will." So, for the existentialist, all life— that which is past and that which is yet to be—lies in this determining moment (the deciding existens) with the challenge: "As you will ... as you will."

This present willing is that which closes all painful moments within the historic continuum and prohibits fantastic fantasies toward the future. This determining work, this willing, is the result of centering the psyche within the parentheses of each succeeding existential moment. It is quite like viewing a movie film by an editor, one frame at a time. In each frame, the apparent movement of the picture is frozen so one may see the individual, still photographs that make up what we perceive as movement. The centering, the stillness, of each life frame (the existens) is that exercise necessary for existential happiness and peace. It doesn't just happen, but it is the result of meditation, faith, and intense behavior modification that we must learn within each succeeding moment along the continuum, in that process which is called becoming. Bedeviled by ancient wrongs, perceived attacks, and cruel injustices and plagued by a rapacious greed, many people find the present untenable.

But it is exactly the present that is important; there is nothing else. One cannot live in the past. It is gone and forever irretrievable—even the memories of that past are suspect, as we have previously discussed. There is no way of accessing future moments without living through the moment that is. The poet Christopher Dryden's quatrain expresses this existence in the present moment.

Happy the man and happy he alone,
He who can call today his own;
He who, secure within, can say,
"Tomorrow, do thy worst, for I have lived today."

Moses, the ancient leader of the Israelites prior to Canaan, while tending his father-in-law's sheep, saw a bush on fire, but the bush was not consumed. Turning aside for a closer look at this marvel, he was warned by a voice to not approach and to remove the shoes from his feet for the ground on which he was standing was holy ground. The voice instructed Moses that he, with his brother Aaron, was to lead the Israelites out of Egypt and into the promised land.

Moses replied, "Whom shall I say has sent me?"

From the bush, the voice of God spoke again, "I Am that I Am. Tell the children of Israel I Am has sent you."

The verb *I am* in Hebrew, a form of the verb to be may be translated as "to exist, to live" (all in the present tense of that verb).

The story is framed as a theological indication of the suprachronos logos, the "beyond time-ness of God." Time is the concession to humanity's limited ability to comprehend movement through geography. For instance, as Grover on *Sesame Street* instructs us, I cannot be "over here" and "over there" at the same time. One can only understand repositioning within space as a consequence of differences in time. I can be over here and *then* over there because the first takes place in one instance in time, and the second takes place in another. God, on the other hand, is the Eternal Present. He is history, He is the now, and He is the future. "The same yesterday, today, and forever" (Hebrews 13:8).

Christian theology, without this existentialist viewpoint, finds great difficulty explaining the Christos within history. Those from the more conservative theologizing academia wish to preserve Jesus's birth, death, and resurrection inside a historic framework. Such identification within history begs the question of His soteriological efficacy. Only that which is outside the damning milieu can affect any rescue.

An illustration may help at this point: A father and son are walking through a swamp. Suddenly, they are trapped in a pit of quicksand. The son begs his father to pull him from the enclosing morass, but there is no place for the father's feet to gain purchase to extricate himself, let alone his son. A hunter, passing nearby, answers their cries for help, but in his haste, he is also trapped by the quicksand. Being near the edge, he can reach a branch of a tree to pull himself to firmer ground beside the pit. Using his outsideness and the branch as a tool, he is able to pull both victims from the quagmire.

It is the eternal extratemporalness of God and the Christ that provides us our soteriological relief. An adequate understanding of good psychology informs us that a therapist may counsel any client only to the level of his or her own understanding. In education, we assume the teacher is beyond the understanding of the student; otherwise, no learning is possible. The superior medical training of the doctor and nurse rescues us from illness and disease. In each of these mundane illustrations, it is the *aboveness* or *outsideness* of each professional that provides the leverage for rescue.

Only an existential understanding of Deity and the Christos provides us with sound theological answers. The Christological events were not, in the strictest of senses, historical happenings, but they are the saving experiences for those to whom they continually happen. The appearances of Jesus, following His Crucifixion were real events to those to whom He appeared: Mary of Magdala (Mark 16:9), several other women (Matthew 28:9), Peter (1 Corinthians 15:5), the ten apostles without Thomas (John 20:19–24), the eleven apostles with Thomas present (John 20:26–28), two unknown disciples on the Emmaus Road (Luke 24:29–31), seven disciples while fishing (John 21:1–14), Paul (Acts 9:1–6, 1 Corinthians 15:8). They became real events to those who, upon hearing these first witnesses, had faith to believe. Those same original witnesses communicated their existential seeing of the resurrected Jesus, now the Christos, through their writings in Holy Scripture and through the ancient creeds of the church. They become real to us, in each present tense, through our willing faith.

In Greek, the word *pisteo*, usually translated "to believe," derives its meaning from the noun *pistis*, "faith," and is an active verb: "to faith." I faith these events; therefore, I can believe them. Faith, in this sense, is a willed act to which belief is subsequent. In this rational sequence, belief is not an acceptance of what was or what I have been told; it is the consequent result of my faithing particular events in each existential moment. The appearances of Jesus, therefore, are real for me, not because of historical veracity but because the ancient witnesses convinced my mind their reports were real for them in their existent moment. The reality and importance of those events become true for me in this moment of my existence through my faithing belief.

Let me interject that faith is not unique to theology or religion. Without faith, nothing can be projected from the now into any future. This is also true for science, business, and politics. In chemistry, for instance, scientific facts are the result of consistent observation. If I place a copper penny in a test tube partially filled with sulfuric acid, the resultant fact is free hydrogen gas is released, a fact I can prove by lighting the mouth of the test tube (the chemical formulation is: $H_2SO_4 + Cu = CuSo_4 + H_2$). According to scientific principles established by observed uniformity of reaction, I may confidently state that this chemical formula has always reacted in this way. But any prediction, that this will happen in any future instant is, a statement of faith.

The scientific fact that the moon revolves about the earth through a twenty-eight-day cycle is stated because of its historically observed uniformity, but to state this will happen in any future time is a statement of faith.

Millions of dollars are raised for political campaigns to ensure through publicity, and other less appropriate methods, a particular candidate's election. The promises made concerning political stances, economic policies, and foreign affairs are not statements of fact; they are statements of faith, which are often misplaced.

The predictions of weathermen, Wall Street analysts, and economic prognosticators, while based on certain uniformities of historic fact, are nothing more than the operation of this faithing. We all know the inaccuracies of weather forecasts, the sudden downturns of stocks on Wall Street, and the disastrous recessions that have followed optimistic economic reports. In all these instances, the projections were based on what appeared to be sound principles. But their organization and application were in error. Too much depended on the past, in anticipation of the eventual satisfaction of economic greed—and too little faithing and living in the present.

Faithing, to faith, is that which carries the existential Christian from this instant, through any or all succeeding instants, through the process of becoming to that one final instant: the Eschaton. In all these illustrations, the operation of faith is based upon the rational examination of a variety of logical factors. To faith, one must will the act of faith to move beyond these principles into those areas where logic cannot reach. The prognostication of events to come, based on those principles, requires the faithing principle. Immanuel Kant believed that reason can take us only so far since reason is a historical and contemporaneous activity; to go beyond the present, one must take the leap of faith.

Emily and I initially tried to communicate, at the inn within, what we believed to be a shared present state. Historical and futuristic thinking erected a wall of miscommunication between him and us. The manager was never in the present. Nothing we said or asked for was important—if it were even heard. What occupied their minds were the blatancies of their needs fired by the angry retaliation they needed to exact as recompense for what they remembered had been done to them historically. While some of this thinking process was subconscious (like the childhood abuse that had arrested their maturation), much was conscious and intentional, a willed choice for perversion.

As the child grows physically, it learns life skills through several venues:

- Fear/respect for parents. The child attempts to do what the parent expects so as not to displease or to ward off punishment.
- Mimicry. The child seeks to imitate the thoughts, actions, and experiences demonstrated by the parents (mobilization, walking, arm movements, gestures, facial expressions, speech, actual words, intonations, sentence structures, and idioms).
- Morality. The child learns through observation of those things that are bad or good—not in some absolute sense, but in a familial sense—through watching closely the parents' moral construction. Traumatic events in early or middle childhood—unreasonable punishment, actual abuse, embarrassment, or parental alcoholism/abuse—arrest physical/chronological maturation and moral development. Alcoholism or alcohol abuse may be encouraged in these early ages by the parents' example; alcoholic aberrancies will eventually show up in the child's early adolescence. If the abuse is severe enough and the moral errancy is blatant enough, the child's moral development is arrested; worse, the child's sense of right and

wrong (the conscience) is obliterated. In classic Freudian terms, only the ego and the id continue to exist. The superego disappears. Such a state is consequently diagnosed as sociopathology, an absence of *knowing* that anything the person decides to do is wrong. The "breaking" of God's law "into pieces."

The inn's manager, the Angel of Death, and her cohorts showed a complete absence of superego with a total lack of boundaries. Their personalities and needs flowed easily across all personal boundary lines and absorbed aspects within other personalities as necessary for their own: others' money is taken as their own and others' praise is accepted as their own. No relationship is safe from their encroachments. They have no conscious thought that they are doing anything *wrong*.

They believed that whatever I had, whatever I could do, should be for them alone. These amoeba-like personality structures lacked any altruistic consciousness—and any consciousness at all. Thoughts concerning environment, social remedies, world/community health were of no interest accept insofar as any one of these, momentarily expounded, might benefit them or their evil schemes. My ex-wife often joined community organizations, not for what she could do for the community, but for what that organization might do for her personal prestige and to gain access to community leaders who might help her further her future tenebrous plans.

For existentialism, the existentialist Christian in particular, childhood abuse and the concomitant moral and psychic arrested states are in the past and affect the present only insofar as they are permitted. Each existential moment is a new opportunity to will closure for all that has been, to forgive ourselves and others, and draw the curtain of forgetfulness over those remembered pasts that can be revisited only at our peril.

The great prayer of Jesus, is replete with illustrations of the existens: "Give us *this* day our daily bread," "Forgive us our sins as we forgive others" (again the present tense of the verb), "Lead us not into temptation but deliver us from evil" (the present imperative of the two verbs), and "For Thine *is* the kingdom."

Jesus, on various occasions, pronounces the *isness* of the soteriological principles: "I Am the resurrection and the life," "The kingdom of God is within you," and "This day this is revealed in your hearing." Following these examples, the existential Christian, having closed any past lives in each succeeding present, until that eschatological moment in which they stand face to face with that great I Am, realizing his journey of becoming is consummated in the presence of the absolute being.

Living in the present requires a total awareness of who we are, where we are in relationship to others, and where we are in relation to the social structures within which we now live; we call this *consciousness*. It is estimated that probably less than 25 percent of the world's inhabitants ever reach this cognitional state. Mired in faulty recollected memories, plagued by a fearsome angst with regard to what the future may require, the main questions of existence are never addressed: Who am I? What am I? Where am I?

Consciousness is not a happenstance; it is a deliberately willed act requiring intense psychic work. Emily consistently reminds me of what a burden it is to be conscious.

More than twenty-three hundred years ago, the author of the small book Ecclesiastes (if Solomon, as the contents might suggest, is the author, then this little booklet dates from the tenth century BCE) intimates that consciousness is difficult. "With much wisdom comes much sorrow; the greater the knowledge; the greater the grief" (Ecclesiastes 1:18). While this might be true, the moral imperative inherent in all the great religious ethical formulations demands our complete awareness of who we are, our place within society, and our rational and empathic reactions to those situations within which we find ourselves. This way of living eventuates the greatest joy.

While the unconscious can, and are content to, wander in the sweet haze of oblivion, the existentially conscious individual is painfully aware of the suffering, injustice, and evil that surrounds him. He is compelled to act in those situations of which he is aware as a soteriological emissary. Martin Luther called this conscious activity in the present "being Christs, like the Christ, to all about you." It was this same perspective that drove Mother Teresa's life. The poor, the retched are only the Christ in one of His desperate disguises. Saint Paul enunciated this full measure of consciousness. "For scarcely for a righteous man will one die: yet peradventure for a good man some would even dare to die. But God commandeth His love toward us, in that while we were yet sinners, the Christ died for us" (Romans 5:7–8).

Moral questions arise for existential Christians: Who is responsible for changing the world? If not you, then who? If not now, when? Existentialist Christians must seriously answer these questions. The process of becoming places the responsibility for being in every existent moment on every existing individual. The maxim, according to Saint James is "to be is to do." Otherwise, being is negated. The New Testament phrases this law of existence in this way: "Therefore to him who knows what it is good to do and does it not, it is sin" (James 4:17). The Old Testament (*Tanakh* in Hebrew) states, "He has shown thee, O man, what is good and what doth the Lord require of thee: Do justice, love mercy, and walk humbly with thy God" (Micah 5:8). All the Hebrew verbs are in the intensive present (imperfect) tense.

To accomplish this state of consciousness, existentialist Christians must forgive and forget all that is past for the self and surrender fantasies concerning the future, while focusing all psychic, psychological, and physical powers intensely within the present tense, the existential now. Each successive instant brings a contentment and satisfaction that cannot be known while encumbered by the past or future and we become like the Christ.

Emily's knitting, which she refers to as "a therapeutic modality" focuses her mind on that existens within which a single stitch is created. Each stitch, in each succeeding instant, is followed by another instant, within which there is created another stitch in a process of intense concentration, satisfaction, and closure through the existential process of becoming, to a completed project (sweater, mittens, or socks). Each existens, each stitch, is complete in itself, releasing the mind from the angst of the past and the anxiety of the future. The question is not "How did we begin?" or "How will the finished article appear?" Instead, we must ask, "Where are we now?" Without this concentration on the present stitch and its perfection, nothing valuable can be achieved. The same is true in her doll making. Each succession of moments is a concentration of single events: the eyes, the hair, the mouth, and the legs. Again, through that process that is *becoming* the doll arises alive.

Ram Dass, in one of his lectures in Atlanta in the early 1990s, related an anecdotal story of an elderly woman in the audience. He described her as wearing a brightly flowered dress, a large hat, and responsible shoes.

Her facial expression was peaceful, her eyes were interested, and she was nodding her head as though she understood the workings of the universe as he presented them. This universe he described was witnessed from the perspective of a consciousness under the influence of mind-altering substances. He was impressed. After the audience was dismissed, this woman approached him and reported that she had, indeed, comprehended.

He asked, "What is your secret?"

She replied, "I crochet."

When I am at the forge, my mind closes itself in meditation to single moments in existent time as the hot coals heat the iron. I watch for the succeeding colors (purple, red, orange, yellow) my grandfather taught me indicated the various forging and tempering temperatures of the metal to be formed: orange for bending and forming and bright yellow—almost white—for forge welding. Through each subsequent instant of heating or hammering, a completed item emerges. It becomes. It is important to read the progression of temperatures, and when a forging heat has been taken (a bright orange), it is equally important in that instant, as the metal is hammered, to feel the movement within the iron and witness what shape and fashion the iron wishes to become. While I may have a general idea of the project I intend to complete, it is only as I work with the iron in each existent instant that both beauty and utility can be achieved.

It is quite like Michelangelo's approach to sculpture. In the marble, he envisions a spirit entrapped, and his work is to release it so it will be what it wants to be. Any approach to true craftsmanship must take into account the existential partnership between creator and that material with which he or she has chosen to work. This same approach is equally valuable in communication and interpersonal relationships.

Contractual psychology teaches us that the expectations and needs of all relating within an existential moment must be recognized, understood, and compromised. For relationships to exist, for communication to happen, some accommodations of needs and aspirations among the interrelating individuals must be made.

Chapter 16

Healing through Faith to Wholeness

THE PSYCHOLOGICAL AND theological processes through which personality changes are made (greed becomes charity, selfishness yields to altruism, evil becomes saintliness) is as difficult as it is simple. It, of course, begins with an acknowledgment that reformation is necessary. Usually, this comes to an individual through some crisis or trauma that overwhelms established defense mechanisms. The moment of this revelation is shocking and painful because it reveals coping mechanisms that are inadequate for the devastation that surrounds the individual.

In the Old Testament, there is a unique story about David and Bathsheba (2 Samuel 11:1–12:7). David, having seduced Bathsheba and murdering her warrior husband, Uriah, took his pregnant concubine as his wife. Later Nathan, the prophet, approached David with this simple story:

> A rich man, with a large flock of sheep, lived near a poor man who possessed a single lamb. A traveler came to the rich man's house at dinnertime. The wealthy man, unwilling to sacrifice one of his many sheep, sent his groom to steal his neighbor's single lamb. At this injustice, David became angry, declaring that the rich man must surely die. In a flash, the prophet turned to face King David, and in a quiet but audible voice, he said, "You are the man."

What shocked David so greatly was not so much that a horrific sin had been committed—but that he was the sinner. It is at this point of recognition that reformation, reclamation, and repentance take place.

Anger, vilification, and attacks no longer serve the psyche in any satisfactory way. The second essential step is a necessary request for help from someone outside the devastated psyche's moral dilemma (clergy, therapist, trusted friend, or family member). Like the individuals in the swamp/quicksand analogy, there is need for help from other persons whose moral stance is outside that which the traumatized individuals are living. Thirdly, there must be a decisive willing that change must take place. The process, then, is behaving in a new way toward change, regardless of the psyche's emotional warnings and needs. Saint Paul says, "We walk by faith to faith" (Romans 1:17).

Another way of saying this is that faithing yields faith. If you do what is right, this will eventuate feelings and emotions for the rightness you are doing. The behavioral theory of cognitive dissonance argues the same tenet: behavior modification may be accomplished by willing a logical and rational action even though the emotions and shallow thought processes argue against such a course. Simply, if we change our behaviors, our attitudes will eventually change to accommodate. It is inconsistent and uncomfortable for sentient beings to behave in ways that are antithetical to the way they think and feel. The movement from self-centeredness to altruism, from selfishness to charity, from hatefulness to saintliness—in each existential moment—is the process of cognitive restructuring. This course of action requires a willing subject with an immediate, intense ability to concentrate. It, too, must be seen as a process of becoming, that is, immediate mind focusing on the corrective behavior followed, in each succeeding instant by reemphatic concentration until that instant within which the emotions and mind coincide.

In Freudian terms, it is the superego using the energy of the ego to thwart the id. This is the rational approach to behavior. In the emotional approach, it is the ego using the blatant energy and narcissism of the id to cancel the superego. This last behavioral structure leads if not to social-pathology, at least to diagnosable neurotic and psychotic tendencies. The existentialist Christian, in addition to the psychological mechanisms just mentioned, adds faith, prayer, and belief in the power of the Holy Spirit as guides and assistants.

If we were to coincide Christian and Freudian terms, we could make some loose equation between the superego and what Christian theology refers to as the "indwelling of the Holy Spirit." In Galatians 5:19–23, Saint Paul mentions both the consequences of psychological evil and the benefits of the Holy Spirit/Superego driven personality: The acts of our baser natures are sexual immorality, impurity, debauchery, idolatry, witchcraft, hatred, discord, jealousy, rage, selfish ambition, envy, drunkenness, and orgies. But the fruit of the Holy Spirit are love, joy, peace, patience, kindness, goodness, faithfulness, gentleness, and self-control.

The writer of the Hebrew tractate in the New Testament says, "Faith is the substance of things hoped for, the evidence of things not seen" (Hebrews 11:1). Another way of translating the Greek is that faith what is needed, and faith will produce the necessary things. Faith is the ability to believe what cannot be seen; the reward of faith is to see that which has been faithed.

Georg Wilhelm Friedrich Hegel (German philosopher 1770–1831) diagrammatically outlined a philosophical process by which individual's progress epistemologically from matter (the earth, their own brutish instincts) toward the ideal (pure truth, the idea [Platonism], God [Hebraic-Christian tradition]). This progression of events, Hegel believed, formed a continuum that he called *becoming*. The schematic outline of this continuum is a series of triads that builds successively on each other (the existentialist would add "in every existent moment"), moving from the unknown to the light of pure reason. Each triad consists of a thesis for which there is an antithesis melded by a synthesis. This synthesis becomes the thesis for the next triad, building continuously (thesis, through antithesis, to synthesis [the new thesis] ad aeternum), finally culminating in that synthesis for which there is no antithesis. The final synthesis, pure existence, can have no antithetical statement since to deny existence is essentially nonexistence (absolute nothingness, the complete absence of being), which cannot be conceived or mentioned. This philosophical structure, as we apply it to Christian existentialism, helps identify the stages (immediate instants) of cognitive dissonance that progressively create a perfected life by willed behavior modification.

Some philosophers like Carl Marx and Albert Camus, turn the Hegelian, triadic structure upside down. Beginning with pure idea (God, pure reason), they find rational possibilities in nothingness. They eventually arrive at pure matter (the absence of any spirit). Such philosophies, pessimistic to the extreme, are the foundation of both Socialism and Communism. Even Søren Kierkegaard, known as the Melancholy Dane, while rejecting the conclusions of Marx and Camus, still finds the ends of his philosophy gloomy and absurd. Indeed, Kierkegaard, finds himself on the "horns of a dilemma" needing to postulate both *isness* and *nothingness* within the same triad, the only synthesis for which is the action of what he calls the absurd (believing that both existence and nonexistence occur simultaneously for the existentialist). Pessimism is derived in every moment, since any joy or exuberance within an existent instant is immediately tempered by the throes of nonexistence.

Tomorrow will dawn,
Again, tomorrow
As it has dawned
Since time began.
And there will be more tomorrows
Anticipation and realization,
Repetition and confirmation,
In endless cycles of waiting,
And finding—and remembering.
Between the beginnings and the endings,
Among the daydreams and the nightmares,
In the midst of darkness and disclosure,
Bornings and the dyings,
Little things filter in
To fill the hollow spaces
Within the tomorrows:
Tiffany diamonds,
Tiny, shining suns,
For sale:
Gold filigree rings
And garden swings
That pale.
Doublets and gherkins,
Stained by firkins
Of ale;

White, fuzzy cotton,
Piled high, shocking
To bale.
Stuffed little creatures
Whose soft little features,
Female and male,
Curdle and soften,
More often
Than not,
Our pessimistic tale.
Yet these are the things,
Simple rememberings,
That never fail
To amuse us,
Entertain and bemuse us,
Right down to each psychic entrail.
Are these real?
Or do they only feel
Substantial, these ethereal
Little interludes
Betwixt the waiting and the waiting—again?
Diffident, vaporous, etudes
From some distant refrain
Deluding our minds delusions?
Dedicated confusions
Rendering what is so that it cannot be,
What cannot be so as
To be the only reality.
And this, this, the only sorrow:
As it has been, so will it be tomorrow.

Christian existentialism is optimistic and full of joy in every instant. Joy, in this sense, is a willed response to any situation (good or bad.)

> Consider it a pure joy my brothers, when you face trials
> of any kind, because you know that trials test your faith

developing perseverance. Perseverance finishes its work
and we become mature and complete, lacking nothing.
(James 1:2–5)

One cannot dictate the situations within which one finds the self. But each of us can determine our responses to that situation. Pain exists, evil may surround us, illness may plague us, but it is our response to all these that determines how they will affect us. Pain is secondary to a variety of physical conditions, but concentration on that discomfort and fear in anticipation of the next wave of distress only exacerbate the intensity of the individual's perceptions.

Surviving painful situations is a matter of will that takes place in each existential moment. Saint Paul wrote to the Church at Philippi: "Be anxious for nothing, but in everything, with prayer and supplication make your requests known to the Lord, and God will grant you peace through Our Lord Jesus the Christ" (Philippians 4:6–7). Whenever the body or mind experiences stress due to work, relationships, illness, or loss, it is the product—not of any of those problems—but of our anxious and fearful responses to them.

A man goes to work every day as he has for twenty years; nothing has changed in his basic routines except his escalating boredom and impatience with his job or career. Psychologically exasperated by what he perceives is not happening in his workday, he is tired and irritable with the family when he arrives home. He complains that his inability to get along with family, coworkers, and friends is the result of stress in his career. It is, however, not the career but his pessimistic interpretations of his everyday existence. A new family, new friends, or new job will not make a difference, but new attitudes regarding all these will change the level of stress he experiences. This is not happenstance; rather, it will be the culmination of a willed choice to find in everything, in each moment, something of joy and peace, a direct gift of God.

William Ernest Henley, in his poem "Invictus," captures this existential ability of willed response.

Out of the night that covers me,
Black is the pit from pole to pole,

I thank, whatever Gods may be,
For my unconquerable soul.
In the fell clutch of circumstance,
I have not winced nor cried aloud,
Under the bludgeonings of chance,
My head is bloody, but unbowed.
For beyond this vale of wrath and tears,
Lies but the horror of the shade,
Yet the passage of the years,
Finds and shall find me unafraid.
It matters not how straight the gate,
Nor, yet, how charged with punishment the scroll;
I am the Master of my fate,
I am the Captain of my soul.

Chapter 17

Divine Intervention

T HERE IS INFINITELY more of the spirit of "Invictus" about real life than there is of that essence of self-pity and emotional inertia seen far too often in the inhabitants of our society. On a lighter note, in a poem I wrote some years ago, this same inviolable approach to life is extolled:

> Don't worry; it's never your fault;
> Someone else is to blame.
> Responsibility shouldn't concern you;
> That's everyone else's game.
> Do what you want, say what you will;
> It's your right, it's the law.
> Should problems arise, angers explode,
> It's everyone else's faux pas.
> Something wrong? Sue in the court!
> Turn everyone inside, about,
> Make "them" pay; make "them" squirm;
> It's better than finding you out.
> Blame your parents, your sitters, your school;
> It's the fault of your peers, your pills, your shrink.
> Whine over their faults, all you have lost,
> Wallow in pity, depression; take a drink.
> Or get on your feet, spit in their eye;
> It's your life after all.
> Claim victory or defeat by the strength of your soul,
> Standing crippled and hurt—but tall.

It is by this philosophy I have tried to live. This regimen would become absolutely necessary in the fifteen weeks of my hospitalization. On the last Tuesday in May, the voices—together with the ranting and ravings of my tormentors—would be silenced for me. At two o'clock in the afternoon, I had a massive heart attack. The chest pains, although familiar, did not respond to my usual therapies: deep breathing, hot water, and meditation. Finally, I asked Emily to call the paramedics. The next hours and days are very much a blur. I only remember promising Emily that I would not leave her.

The ambulance rides to the emergency room and subsequently to the hospital form a distant part of my consciousness. The cold sterility of the operating room forced its way through my medicated stupor into my consciousness. I prayed simply but intensely: "God, I've made Emily a promise. I need your help to fulfill it." Then darkness.

I woke up three days later, strapped in my bed, with tubes from every orifice. I heard Emily talking. I wanted desperately to see her, but I had an endotracheal tube attached to a respirator. I couldn't speak; I had no voice. I tried to sign to the bedside nurses, pointing to the door, trying to indicate that I needed to see my Emily.

Whether they comprehended or not, the nurses appeared not to understand—until they saw my agitation level rising. I struggled against the bindings at my hands and feet. Worried that I might injure myself, they went to find the doctor, and in the process, they informed Emily that I was awake. She was finally there, softly stroking my hand. She whispered to me that everything was fine and that she understood. She had telephoned my eldest son, and he told Emily he would soon be with us. He had engaged an army to pray for my recovery.

With Emily at my side, my anger and agitation subsided. I knew, in that instant, that we would make it. I knew God had heard and answered my prayers. He had finalized the verdict: my place was not in some ethereal kingdom—but with Emily and my family. I also realized, in that moment, my pathway was leading me moment by moment (existentially understood) separating myself from all my history and anticipating nothing of the future. I knew that I must live intensely minute by minute within the shadow of Him who is known as the great I Am. Much of the next weeks melded into pain, procedures, and small steps that would eventually lead to the beginning of recovery.

A drama surrounded me. Emily and my children informed that I might not live, never communicated my prognosis. Blissfully, within the isolation of my prayers and my existentialism, I simply sought to *be*, and that was enough.

During this time, my philosophy was not perfect. As each day dawned and some new surgical procedure was announced, I allowed myself, however briefly, to dwell in the anticipatory anxiety of despair. Emily would ask me what was wrong. She held my hand as I searched my innermost psyche to discover the disturbing submergence of my faith. I prayed the De Profundis: "Out of the depths have I cried unto Thee; Lord, hear my voice" (Psalm 130:1).

The calm of the presence of God would descend upon me, and I knew I needed only face that one moment—the rest was in the hands of God. It was these moments, the absolute *existential now*, that calmed my soul and made the facing of any procedure, any pain possible. The miracle is not mine; it is the actions of an infinite God reaching into my finiteness and the caring love of my Emily. She was at my side night or day, whenever she was permitted or could slip by the vigilant eyes of the nurses. Her absolute constancy exhausted her and gave me strength.

The nurses and the medical personnel did not understand the special relationship that exists between Emily and me. They often chased her from my room on the pretext that she and I needed quiet time to rest. My protracted illness forced the incorporation of the staff into our extended family, and their concern made Emily sometimes feel as though she had become their project. When they suggested she go home and take a nap, she would reply, "I can't sleep at night. How would I ever be able to sleep during the day!" They seemed not to comprehend that we rested better, calmed more effectively within the other's presence. Until my progress moved to the rehabilitation phase, no one could predict if Emily would be able to take me home alive. Only recently did she confess not wanting to miss any moments we could have together. Being separated, if we had only a short time left, made no sense to her.

Emily's exhaustion, all too evident, was cause for constant concern. She was expending enormous amounts of physical energy caring for me in the hospital and emotional energy worrying when we were apart. As helpless as I was—and as difficult as it was to see her tiredness—I came to know I needed to accept the gift of her presence. The knowledge of her prayers and constant caring buoyed me during the long, sleepless, and lonely hours of the night. With her, I would pray, meditate, and wait for the expected presence of God. I was never disappointed.

Many of the happenings in the first few weeks after my surgery come back to me now in short scenes and nebulous images. Each moment of each day was simply a challenge to feel and live within that instant without anticipation or its concomitant anxiety.

At the beginning of each new day, I waited for the hallway lights to be turned brighter and for the vagrant rays of light from the outside; the morning brought the imminent arrival of my wife. Besides my thoughts, prayer, and meditations, the night was filled, as any hospital is, with sounds, voices, medications, procedures, and sometimes just a nurse with a flashlight shining brightly on my face to see if I were asleep.

Four-thirty in the morning brought the inevitable and ubiquitous portable x-ray machine. Hard plastic cases containing x-ray film were maneuvered, repositioned, moved between my shoulder blades and my hips, and adjusted for just the right picture. This inflicted pain; the simple—but, to me, seemingly unnecessary—movements to arrive at a good x-ray should have been made with more expedition than I witnessed. This intrusion was usually followed by my bath. The ablution ritual ran the gamut from a dry cleaning (a powdered cloth waved innocuously over my naked frame) to full contact massage that left me breathless and exhausted. Medications, shift changes, and the explorations of new doctors and new nurses about my physique usually occupied four to five hours. During that time, regardless of when Emily arrived, I was not permitted to see her. It enraged me, and I was a nonverbal communicant.

About three weeks into my recovery, I experienced the most agonizing night. I had been resting comfortably when, at about eight o'clock, extraordinarily sharp pains enveloped my stomach and abdomen. Gripping the sides of my bed and praying as hard as I knew how to pray, I pressed my call button. I was able to communicate to the nurse that I wanted Emily, needed Emily.

The next hours were a nebulous fog of movement and action—in the midst of which was my Emily. Each moment, I knew I needed only to trust her and the God in whom I had put my faith with an intense concentration on "living through" each succeeding painful event. Eventually, I awakened from my stupor and was told I had been sleeping. Although the pain was gone, haunting memories of its intensity began to creep into my consciousness, bringing the anticipatory anxiety of a reoccurrence. Fighting back these evil encroachments from the past and the infiltrations from the future, I tried to relax into the comfort and peace of my present painlessness. I prayed for wisdom and strength to center my mind on this existential task.

As I reflect on those experiences, I am reminded of the three disciplines that afforded me the necessary training to concentrate my mental and psychological powers within each extant moment:

The first was my training as a priest; the repetitive prayers ordained for the canonical hours, committed to memory, became the intercessory framework for my life. These are the prayers of Christians, gleaned from two millennia of soteriological experience; they are both comfort and guidance in times of stress. These prayers, the church has collected and ordered to be prayed during the ten prayer divisions of each day:

- Prime, midnight
- Terse, 3:00 a.m.
- Matins, 6:00 a.m. or daybreak
- Lauds, 9:00 a.m.
- Psalter, noon
- Vespers, 3:00 p.m.
- Sext, 6:00 p.m.
- Nones, 9:00 p.m.
- Compline (the last service of the day) after 9:00 p.m. and before midnight

Because of these daily habits I practiced over the years since my ordination, prayers have become easy and instantaneous safety nets for my life.

Secondly, while learning and mastering the discipline of Tae Kwon Do—with its emphasis on meditation, self-control, and the marshalling of one's inherent energies to be released in a momentary burst—prepared me for any exigency I might face.

Thirdly, as a psychologist, I worked with clients suffering from addictive diseases. I incorporated the twelve-step program of Alcoholics Anonymous into their ongoing therapy and the important lesson of living one moment at a time (an existential departure from their mantra, one day at a time). Other catchphrases from AA and other self-help programs assisted me in focusing and centering my emotions in many difficult moments: Keep it simple. Don't sweat the small stuff—and everything is small stuff. Yield to your higher power.

All these habits, mantras, and behaviors, consistently practiced, became my bulwark against the needless expenditure of inconsistent energy and calmed me in the most difficult situations. Because of my daily commitment to these practices, I was afforded the ability to marshal their forces in the midst of my illness. The behavioral assists are available and valuable only insofar as they are consistently and instantly in practice; they are part of the existential continuum of becoming and therefore instantly practicable.

This existentialist mantra takes us to the essence of the universe:

- Nothing can be that never has been.
- Nothing can become except what is.
- Nothing will be except what is becoming.

Applying the laws of physics, matter can neither be created nor destroyed. At the beginning (creation or big bang), all the energy of the cosmos came into being. The changes, transformations, divisions, and mutations occur, but these provide nothing new, only borrowings, splittings, and changings. In philosophy, art, medicine, and science, we "discover" nothing new—only new combinations, rephrased conceptions, and redrawn spatial outlines. We do not create. New ideas are the mirages assembled by our ability to rebel, forget, reforge, and restate.

The problem is that too many people believe themselves capable of creating new essences within the universe. Our government colludes in this mistaken arrogance, having established a very busy patent office with the express intent of guaranteeing that each person's special invention cannot be copied. But every invention borrows from all the past inventions and is simply a restatement of what already has been. It is rather, for us, who wish to live existentially, to divest ourselves of this blatant arrogance, concentrating only on what we are capable of understanding in the immediate present.

The Christian Church has fallen prey to this egotistical theological thinking. From the ancient Gnostics down to present Fundamentalists and monolithic church teachings, Christians have believed in the uniqueness and catholicity of their own peculiar confessional stances. In reality, these isolationist theologies are only an expression of adolescent jealousy. Each person, in each moment, knows some partial truths, sufficient revelations to live confidently in each instant, but owns no superior theological prerogatives. The primitive church at Jerusalem in the First Church Council (45 CE, Acts 15:22–35) decided that Christianity must not be exclusive or arrogantly believe that any sect or division of the church is custodian of the entire truth. As there ought not to be patents for "inventions," neither is there sole proprietorship on that which is ultimately and totally true.

This arrogance and predestinational Calvinistic theology are the servants of unconsciousness. The presumptuous belief that an individual is all-knowing and the only one privy to the truth—the Christian existentialist must realize this cannot be a valid approach to life. In every epistemological instant, there are countless thinkers thinking their thoughts with partial, external verification, but they are equally true even in their partiality.

As I lay in my hospital bed, thoughts mingled with emotions and changed instantly with the experiential and existential information that was constantly arriving, requiring cognition. I could not live in the past; there was no time to sift through unreliable memories.

I could not allow future anxiety to cloud my perceptions. Whatever would be would be—regardless of my angst. Every moment was enough. Filling that moment with whatever joy or pain it offered made the "handling" of each moment possible. Sometimes, when new situations were proposed, and I felt I had "enough," my anxiety became palpable and apparent, my faith at a low ebb. In those moments, Emily would recall me from my self-centered pity with simple reminders, encouragement, and prayers; the existentialist train moved from its siding and back onto the main track.

Each second of the fifteen hospitalized weeks was an opportunity to practice my faith and depend on my God. Through prayer and meditation,

I was able to walk through that difficult journey. Emily, the doctors, the nurses, and the auxiliary staff told me that I always looked so peaceful—and that only I knew something that was making the course of my illness unexplainable.

Prognosis is dependent upon how many organ systems are failing. With only one organ system involved, there is a 60 percent chance of recovery. When two organs fail, a favorable prognosis decreases to 40 percent. When failure encompasses four or more systems, the mortality rate nears 100 percent.

Three weeks postop, I was in multi-organ failure. I had an ileus (GI failure), I was unable to breathe without the assistance of a respirator (pulmonary failure), my urinary output had all but stopped, and my blood tests showed an increase in BUN and creatinine levels (renal failure). My heart function was dependent upon high doses of IV medication, without which my life could not be sustained, and the doctors were not at all encouraged. I was, however, always alert and oriented, my ability for cognition never decreased, and my long- and short-term memory remained intact. That was the ray of hope—the reason that the staff and I stayed committed to my recovery.

Emily would often ask me if I had had enough, if I were too tired to go on. My answer was always an unequivocal "no." There was no manner of suffering I could not endure if it meant remaining in this incarnation with my Emily. My commitment to living each moment, experiencing each pain, each joy, each feeling of peace allowed this process to proceed through my illness to my continued recovery and the anticipation of my days filled with the treasures of my life. To use my blacksmith tools at my forge to create the miracles that spring from the metal. To reemploy my wood-sculpting chisels to free the soft-flowing forms begging to emerge. To be surrounded by my books filled with linguistic and archeological adventures. To experience the joy and exhilaration of translating the Bible from Hebrew or Greek. To decipher the codes of the Etruscan or Mayan languages. To learn a brand-new dialect. To have the privilege of saying the Mass and preaching the love of the Christ. To travel to Scotland, the home of my grandmother. To sleep in my own bed. To sit in front of a fireplace. To hear the rain and the music of Mozart. To drive a car. To feel the sun on my body. To help my granddaughter with her homework. To share a meal with my family. To take a shower. To take a deep breath without a respirator. To walk without a cane. And to be alone with my Emily in the silence of the night.

There were no tunnels, bright lights, or meetings with my ancestors, but there is a profound knowledge that I am loved and watched over by a God that holds me in His hands and wants only good for me.

My guide and comfort comes from Romans 8:35–39:

> Who shall separate us from the love of the Christ? Shall tribulation or distress, or persuasion, or famine, or nakedness, or peril, or sword? … Nay, in all these things we are more than conquerors through Him who loves us; for I am persuaded neither death nor life, nor angels, or principalities nor powers, nor things of the past nor things yet to come, nor height, nor depth, nor anything else in all of creation shall be able to separate me from the love of God, that is in Christ Jesus our Lord.

This is my faith.

Epilogue

I knew the day might come
When I had to face my life without you.
But I had no idea how totally and completely I would love
And be in love with you.

WILLIAM LIVED FOURTEEN more years and died in my arms from complications from his heart attack. During those years, he lived his faith courageously and in thanksgiving. Saint Francis said, "Pray every minute and only when necessary use words." William prayed unceasingly and touched the lives of thousands through his selfless acts of kindness and generosity of spirit. He lived a life so extraordinary it proved to me the existence of the Divine; who else could have created such an extraordinary soul?

It is only through God's grace that we shared such an amazing love. It carried us through our many lives together on our way to *becoming*. I hold on to God's promise we will be reunited once again.

Our story doesn't end with William's death. Our irretrievable and unconditional love pierces the thin veil between here and the other side. It transcends this earthly plane to a love that can only be described as breathtaking and ethereal. A love ordained by God granted us every lifetime together—if only for a brief moment.

A mist of morning clouds opened to reveal a memory of a past life, a life in which we shared one of those brief moments. He was a Northern military officer, and I was a battlefield nurse crouched on the ground while caring for a seriously wounded soldier.

Gettysburg
July 3, 1863

Bullets raging around me,
Deafening noise,
Mangled bodies,

Blood-soaked earth,
Screams of agony.
I, desperate to ease the suffering.
Suddenly, a hand stretched out to help me stand.
Then silence …
We stood alone, together,
A single glance,
A single minute captured all of our shared lives,
Together.
We knew this was not to be this time,
But in this glance, a promise,
And
Flooding memories of our love we know so well.

The metaphysical doors have opened to the next dimension. William's presence is always around me. Each morning and afternoon, we travel back and forth to work. I chatter about my day and share the sadness of his physical absence.

He sends me images—the symbol of the yin and yang encircled with God's bright light, reassuring me he is near and what a glorious day it will be when I return home to him. He promises to be waiting for me and to be by my side and carry me to heaven in his loving arms and into those of our Creator.

He shows me butterflies, dragonflies, and soaring hawks flying over the car as answers to my many questions. It was no coincidence; a message could not have been clearer, when perched on a pole next to me was one of those majestic hawks, monitoring my conversation with a male friend. Awakening to Stevie Wonder's "I Just Called to Say I Love You" playing in my mind but knowing all too well it was a message from his heart to mine.

Through a medium, I asked if the answers I heard were truly his. "You are my heart," he said. "You feel the words in your heart, and you know they are from *my* heart."

From our first encounter, it was clear he was such an advanced soul. It was concerning to me that he would be on a higher level in heaven when we were called home. Teasingly, I would say, "God will surely be sending you on missions, leaving me behind." Waving goodbye, I will remind you I will be waiting. "Please hurry back to me."

"I am never leaving you again," he would say, vehemently shaking his head. "You will be going with me on every mission. You are every bit as advanced as I. We have much to do, you and I, for the glory of God."

His words, the absoluteness of his knowing, always struck me as curious. I believed myself a mere mortal in comparison. William was brilliant, a self-contained soul. Infused knowledge poured into him almost constantly from the mind of God. Needing only minimal human interaction, his pride and extraordinary intellect kept him isolated—until me. He fostered a subtle arrogance and assuredness not noticed by those encircling his external world. Suddenly, without warning, his defenses, his pride, and his confidence failed him. His arrogance evaporated literally overnight the day we met.

"I have met my equal; we are the same," he proclaimed.

In twenty-five years, we never ran out of things to talk about. Quietly sitting together working on even the most mundane of projects was a joy for which we were grateful. Stressors were always met with us saying, "Everything is okay because we have each other."

William's last years were filled with excruciating back pain and multiple medical complications secondary to his heart attack. In spite of his pain, his handsome countenance was always peaceful. Harsh words never crossed between us. I was always at his side during his subsequent hospitalizations, and they were never brief. Each one confined him to months of care, and additional physical rehabilitation was always necessary in order for him to regain his strength. I was terrified as he became weaker, worrying my ability to care for him at home might be compromised, but each time, together, we made it work.

For the last three years, he suffered the indignities of dialysis. Treatments left him weak, nauseated, and with a corresponding increase in his back pain. He paid little attention to his illness and had no understanding of his physical limitations. He was always pushing himself to exhaustion.

His insidious physical decline seemed to escape me until the last six months when he could no longer be out of bed without my assistance. I loved caring for him. Bathing him and caring for his wounds was a devotional and spiritual journey. The trust he had in my abilities and the sacredness of this shared intimacy was a spiritual connection transcending the physical and flowed directly into every niche of our lives. It was my delight to see the excitement on his face, like that of a tail-wagging golden retriever, as I walked through the door after my day's work.

His death took me by surprise. I seemed to be the only one in the world who didn't know the extent of his illness and that he was going to die. Two months before his death, I was experiencing shortness of breath from exertion, chest pain radiating down my left arm and into my jaw. I was nauseated and had night sweats. My family history is positive for sudden cardiac death at a young age. Dying first was my expectation. I prayed to stay alive until he could no longer. He often said he could tolerate any manner of suffering if it meant staying with me even one minute more. My prayers were answered, and I remain lost in this luminal space, brokenhearted to have been left behind.

My grief is unbearable at times. Unable to escape the profound sorrow, I am imprisoned in my body. My soul pushing against my mortal coil fighting to be released, like an infant's erratic movements trying desperately to figure out how to fit its expansive soul into this tiny human space.

He is my love, my life. I never needed anyone else. His absence renders me blind without orientation in this physical dimension. He was swaddling clothes, wrapping me in safety, comfort, love, and strength. With each passing day, the entrenched denial phase of grief wears a little thinner as my psyche is forced to face increasingly more of the blatant truth. His shoes are where he left them as I try to fool myself with the disbelief he will be coming home soon to wear them.

Removing myself from this life is not an option, although I can't deny I have stood on the precipice of insanity and begged God to take me home with the frustration of a child throwing a tantrum. My emotional pain mocks me and dares me to set myself free. He is out of reach to soothe me, wrap his loving arms around me, speak softly, and tell me all will be okay. There are no hands to dry my tears or lips to kiss my sadness away.

If heaven is my lifetime achievement reward for completing my purpose, then interrupting this incarnation will eventuate the consequence of returning to life to repeat this pain. I would be separated from my William, the very suffering I am praying to avoid. This is unimaginable.

Only my faith assures me I am not alone. I know I am surrounded by God's love and the eternal presence of Father and Mother God, my angels, the Christ, my spirit guides, those I have loved who have gone before me, and—most of all—my William. It is this awareness that allows peace to descend upon me. I remind William and God each morning that I am one day closer to returning home to them.

When we met, our souls' recognition was immediate.

"I have been looking for you all of my life," he uttered within six days of our reunion. "Let's pretend it is next year. Will you marry me?"

"Probably," I blurted out. I thought, *I don't know who said that.*

In four months, we did marry. I had only two conditions: (1) he would agree to be a vegetarian and (2) every day he would say, "I adore you." Our vows were simple. "I will love you forever—and no other." In twenty-five years, he never failed. Each day, I still hear from his heart: "I love and adore you." We had a silly ritual when I came home from work. William would ask, "Have I told you I adore you today?"

I would say no—but of course he had—so I could hear him tell me once again.

As William was an Anglican priest, his most treasured possessions were the sacred vestments he wore when offering the Mass. Those robes were my gift to him and God, my handmade works of art that surrounded him with my loving embrace each time he donned them. His attachment to them transcended to heaven. No one was permitted to touch them as I helped him robe for Mass.

When fully vested, William was transformed. His six-feet-two-inch, 230-pound presence moved through God's grace and gentleness. He knew the Liturgy by heart, so the words came directly from the voice of his soul to the ears of God and those fortunate enough to witness this loving conversation. Homilies were meditations of God's love about which we are always engulfed and our need to be in service to others. William believed and lived the Gospel of Saint James for which his blacksmith shop was named. Faith without good works will not save a man ... that is sin.

He confided to me that he knew it was strange his attachment to his chasubles followed him to the other side, but there was no question of his desire to have them cremated and returned to the earth and the winds. I carried out his wishes, and they were released to him on a beautiful autumn day. He received my gift of love to be recreated in the dimension in which he now resides. It was my sacrificial offering given with great devotion to the God I trust—my offering to and for His faithful servant

William, who in spite of his brilliance and many talents walked humbly and quietly on this physical plane. The following morning, my husband appeared to me robed in the chasuble of white silk, with gold embroidered galloons lined with gold lamé. Surrounded by a magnificent white light, his hands were raised, as he would do during the consecration of the host.

With no guarantee, each minute may be our last here on earth. It was important I quickly complete his request. I worried that if I should die, someone could find these precious belongings without any understanding of their importance and specialness. It might be decided to give them away or tragically throw them away. My sadness was in not the conflagration but the recognition that if they no longer existed on this earth, I must then accept William was never coming home again.

This project has been both freeing and excruciatingly difficult. Re-reading our story meant tearing open old wounds and reliving, alone, a time I had tried desperately to forget and forgive. William's love for me and his God, his kindness, and his brilliance leap from every page. In my memories, his visage is that of a strong, robust, and healthy man. With that image, his illness and suffering fade from my mind. It is nearly impossible for me to understand why God took him home and why he is no longer with me. William's life purpose was completed, and we agreed before we incarnated that I would remain ... just possibly to share our story with you.

On this final leg of our life's journey, if it is possible, I have fallen in love with him all over again. My heart is always open to the extraordinary love we share and in knowing I will spend eternity with him in the stone cottage with a huge fireplace he has prepared for us. And so it is.

www.ingramcontent.com/pod-product-compliance
Lightning Source LLC
Chambersburg PA
CBHW020522290526
45786CB00002B/720